POWER AND THE POWERS

POWER AND THE POWERS

Walter Brueggemann

Conrad L. Kanagy
editor

Fortress Press
Minneapolis

POWER AND THE POWERS

31 30 29 28 27 26 25 1 2 3 4 5 6 7 8 9

Library of Congress Control Number: 2025023075 (print)

Cover image: Compilation of abstract digital painting stock images, Unsplash
Cover design: John Lucas

Print ISBN: 979-8-8898-3631-5
eBook ISBN: 979-8-8898-3632-2

CONTENTS

PREFACE

This is the sixth in a series of books that have emerged since May 2022, each composed of short essays originally written by Walter Brueggemann from 2020 to 2025. The essays reflect Brueggemann at the top of his prophetic game. It's hard to imagine that like the wine of Jesus's first miracle, the best of Brueggemann would be saved for the end of his days. But in reading essay after essay, it is hard to argue otherwise. In each, Walter brings to bear the biblical exegetical method—for which he was so well known—to one contemporary social issue after another. No one else in the early part of the twenty-first century is doing exactly this kind of contemporary theological and sociological reflection, and, if they are, none as effectively, honestly, and graciously as Brueggemann.

Brueggemann read eight or nine books a week and two newspapers a day and did so for decades. As a child, he read *The Christian Century* even when his pastor father August didn't even. He exhausted the small school library—causing the librarian to bring him books from another town. Walter Brueggemann was a prolific writer, in large part, because he was a voracious reader. But he was not just any reader of just any book. He was, first and foremost, a reader of the biblical text, and that text and its God became the lens, or the frame, through which he saw, interpreted, and prophetically imagined what God just might be up to that the rest of us hadn't ever considered.

Which is why I am so thankful for this book. Saint Paul states in Ephesians 6 that "our struggle is not against blood and flesh but against the rulers, against the authorities, against the cosmic powers of this present darkness, against the spiritual forces of evil in the heavenly." Despite his age—young or old—Walter was always aware of the powers, both natural and supernatural. And more than most of us, he was aware that it is the supernatural powers that can bring the greatest good and do the greatest harm. And unlike most of us, he was unafraid and unashamed to speak against the dark powers and to call us to hope and faith in the God of all the powers. Walter neither lacked courage nor words. Like the saints who preceded him in the German Evangelical Synod tradition and like those Dietrich Bonhoeffer befriended by his tradition, Brueggemann walked by faith and not by sight. And though never called to lie down his life like martyrs before him, I have little doubt he was always prepared to do so.

This book is divided into three parts. Part 1 addresses the many powers that oppress. Part 2 explores the powers that stand with the oppressed against the oppressors. And part 3 includes those essays that acknowledge God as the one power who overcomes all others. This is an arbitrary business, to say the least, for it has never been the lowercase powers that Brueggemann was concerned about. Yes, his essays nearly all address current events and the underlying spiritual powers that are at work within them. But he never gets hung up or overly distressed by these powers or the presence of these powers. The focus in all of his work was the one power before whom every knee will bow and every tongue confess. If you don't yet see the sovereignty of God in every essay that Walter has written you still do not understand Walter Brueggemann. In some ways Walter was fearless. His anxiety about the powers came not from a concern that we will be defeated by them, but that they will create harm for the powerless, that they will reinforce injustice of the marginalized, that they will destroy the beauty of God's creation. In other words, Walter's concern was never for himself but rather for others.

Luther is said to have argued that violence and resistance to the powers are acceptable on behalf of the other. And while Brueggemann said much about his commitment to peacemaking and nonresistance, he, as much as any theologian, stood for the poor, the down and out, the downtrodden, and all who are marginalized by the powers and principalities. He may have left us in doubt about the how, but never about the end of the matter. The pages that follow are no exception to a message that Walter proclaimed to us for sixty-six years.

Part I

THE POWERS THAT OPPRESS

1

GOD WILL NOT BE MOCKED!

Those who mock the poor insult their Maker;
Those who are glad at calamity will not go unpunished.

—Proverbs 17:5; see also 14:21, 22:9, 28:3

THE CLAIMS AND contours of liberation theology are now clearly articulated. In the 1960s and 1970s Roman Catholic theologians, priests, and bishops in Latin America freshly articulated a way to think, speak, and act about social power, social access, and social resources according to the claims of the gospel. That formulation orbits around the phrase, "God's Preferential Option for the Poor." That phrase voices the then scandalous, and still scandalous claim that God is partial to poor people, takes poor people as the object of special care and compassion, and sides with poor people in the class war that the powerful constantly wage against the powerless and resourceless. This interpretive stance, reiterated in many variations, causes scripture to be read very differently, and the mission of the church to be understood and practiced very differently.

The gains for the church in this articulation are immense. At the same time, however, it appears to me that this hermeneutical stance has not much penetrated the thinking, talk, or action of the church, including the Protestant denominations that I know best. It certainly has not impinged upon so-called evangelical churches that continue in their privatistic, otherworldly ways. And it has not much influenced progressive churches that mostly remain adamantly "liberal" in practice, something very different from "liberationist." Because of the slowness of the church's embrace of a liberationist perspective (and in some cases downright resistance), my simple intent here is to call attention to a new book written by Leonardo Boff in his old age, *Thoughts and Dreams of an Old Theologian* (Orbis Books, 2022). The book is readily readable and accessible, and will serve well as a study guide for a congregation. Boff, a Brazilian, from the outset has been among the earliest and most important voices in calling the church to liberationist perspective and practice. That perspective inevitably has led to a critical stance over the imperial propensity of the Roman Catholic Church, a stance against what Boff labels "institutional arrogance." That critical stance has caused Boff (and his brother Clodovis, also a theologian) to be twice silenced by the Vatican under Pope John Paul II. Nonetheless, Boff has continued his courageous work as a theologian and a teacher, who counted Pope Francis as an ally in the work of liberation.

The book, in nine accessible, succinct chapters, sums up a lifetime of research, teaching, and testimony. The outline of the book exhibits Boff following the contours of orthodox Trinitarianism, while he unpacks the tradition in fresh and telling ways. In his brief statement on the intention of Jesus, Boff appeals to the "Our Father" and its petition for "our bread" (45). He identifies "three fundamental and inevitable hungers":

1. The first hunger is for a meeting with Someone good . . . our *kind Daddy* (Abba).
2. The second hunger is the infinite hunger that is never satisfied, the dream of a full meaning for life . . . This comes with the name Kingdom of God.
3. There is yet another hunger . . . This is our daily bread. Without this material basis, talking about our Father and the Kingdom loses its meaning.

Boff summarizes his view of the church that has gotten him into so much trouble with the hierarchy. He pairs the "The Pauline Dimension (Charism) and the Petrine Dimension (Power)" (62). He distinguishes between "power as service" in Jesus and power "as control" in the Petrine Roman model of the church (65). He critiques the self-absorbed power-seeking of the Petrine Church and contrasts it to the "Christianity of Popular Culture" in which the practical faith of the church, with its compassion and social awareness, does not linger over the perspective of the clergy elite. For good reason, Boff welcomes the great Dogmatic Constitution of the Church (*Lumen Gentium*) in Vatican II that saw "the people of God" as moving on in faith without excessive respect for the hierarchical structures of the church (71).

> *The church is not first and foremost a priestly body that creates communities, but the community of those who responded with faith to the call of God in Jesus through his Spirit. The network of these communities forms the People of God because this is the result of a communal, participatory process. . . . Others arise that are more sporadic, but equally important for maintaining the life of the communities; the service of charity, concern for the poor, the promotion of social justice, particularly human, individual, and social rights, and the rights of nature and Mother Earth.* (74)

By contrast,

> *In an ecclesiology that regards the church as a hierarchal society (Petrine), there is no salvation for women in the sense of integration into community services and gifts (Pauline). They are forever marginalized, if not excluded. This state of affairs is incompatible with an ecclesiology that is minimally based on the gospel, which has to incorporate human values because they are also divine values. This is the fundamental reason why we should abandon an exclusively Petrine ecclesiology based on society and hierarchy and build up a Pauline ecclesiology, of community and the People of God.* (75)

Another recurring, crucial accent in Boff's work is his deep concern for the earth in his "ecotheology." He sees in our current thinking and practice two "cosmologies in conflict." One is a "cosmology of conquest, of power as domination" (83). The alternative is a cosmology "gaining strength, the cosmology of transformation and liberation." This latter option received compelling articulation in the encyclical of Pope Francis, *Laudato Si*, "On Care for our Common Home" (2015). Boff pays attention to the processes of living organisms that grow and are transformed at death:

> *Behind all beings acts Fundamental Energy, also called the Nurturing Abyss of all being, which gave origin to the universe and keeps it in being, bringing into existence new beings. The most spectacular of these is the living Earth and we human beings with our component of consciousness and intelligence and the mission to care for the Earth.* (85)

Boff's critique of the cosmology of domination is acute:

> *It started from a false premise that we could produce and consume without limit on a limited planet. The premise also assumes that the fictitious abstraction known as money represents the highest value and that competition and the pursuit of individual interest will result in general well-being. As I described earlier, it takes the form of a cosmology of domination. This cosmology has brought the crisis into the sphere of ecology, politics, ethics, and now economics. The eco-feminists have pointed out the close connection between anthropocentrism and patriarchy, which since Neolithic times has been doing violence to women and nature.* (86–87)

In his penultimate chapter, Boff returns to his most elemental insistence:

> *The supreme and absolute principle of ethics is "Liberate the poor." The principle is absolute because it governs actions*

> *always, in every place and for all. "Free the poor" presupposes (a) the condemnation of a social totality, of a closed system that excludes and produces poor people; (b) an oppressor who produces poor and excluded people; (c) poor people unjustly made poor and so impoverished; (d) taking into account the mechanisms that reproduce impoverishment; (e) the ethical duty to dismantle such mechanisms; (f) the urgency to build an escape route from the system that excludes people; and, finally (g) the obligation to bring about the new system in which all in principle have a role in participation, in justice and solidarity, including nature.*
>
> *This ethics starts from the poor, but it is not just for the poor. It is for all, since no one looking at the face of an impoverished person can feel indifferent; everyone feels concerned. This ethics is fundamentally an ethics of justice, in the sense of restoring the recognition denied to the vast majority and including them in the society from which they feel—and indeed are—excluded.* (109)

At the outset of this piece I have placed a proverb that, well ahead of contemporary ecclesial formulation, had already seen the truth of God's "preferential option for the poor." The proverb asserts that God is particularly attached to, and attentive to, the poor, those who do not and cannot participate effectively in the production-consumption benefits of the economy.

I noticed the term "mock" in the proverb. The "mocking" of the poor is equivalent to insulting or scorning the creator who is the God of the poor. The equation is a remarkable formulation of a deep conviction of the gospel. We will do well to notice, in the context of this proverb, how it is that much church theology and practice has assumed that *God* and *poor* have no connection, as we have fashioned a faith that is individualized and privatized, or that is otherworldly in its escapism. The proverb insists otherwise. It affirms the inevitable, inescapable linkage of God to the economic realities of society, to the political reality that acknowledges not only the presence of the poor, but the production of the poor through the management and manipulation of the economy. This simple equation in the proverb amounts to a critical principle that contradicts our systemic arrangements and summons us to an alternative practice and policy.

The term "mock" in the proverb has led me, perhaps inevitably, to the assertion of the apostle Paul in a quite different context:

> *Do not be deceived; God is not mocked, for you reap*
> *whatever you sow.* (Gal 6:7)

Paul's assertion is an insistence that God's world is morally coherent, that it is a network of causes and effects, of deeds and consequences that are connected and guaranteed by the ordering of the creator. Thus "sow . . . reap." Paul affirms that this linkage, guaranteed by the creator God, cannot be outflanked because it embodies the will of the creator God. God's intention cannot be avoided, and God's will cannot be mocked, either through neglect or defiance.

Consider for a moment this juxtaposition of texts:

> God is not mocked;
> God is insulted by the mocking of the poor.

So yes, God is mocked:

> God is mocked whenever poor people lack food;
> God is mocked whenever the children of poor people must attend inadequate schools;
> God is mocked whenever poor people cannot receive adequate or reliable health care;
> God is mocked whenever poor people are left homeless and without safe shelter;
> God is mocked whenever some in our society lack the security and dignity for full humanness among us.

God is mocked by an economic system of greed that does not notice the poor or excludes the poor from the well-being of the economy. But God will not finally be mocked, because God is in resolved solidarity with poor people. It only remains for us to devise social perspectives, policies, and practices that are congruent with the holy God who is alive, well, and active in the world.

Boff has seen all of this with courageous clarity. Because he is a Roman Catholic teacher and theologian, he has been preoccupied with the way the Roman Catholic Church has colluded in this grotesque distortion of creaturely reality. But of course Boff's concern runs well beyond the Roman Catholic Church. His insistence and anticipation is that the "peoples church" cannot be contained in any fearful ideology and that the church may indeed impact the body politic in transformative ways. Boff concludes his final chapter on spirituality with an appeal to the Eucharist:

> *And now, beloved Earth, I perform the action Jesus performed in the power of his Spirit. Like him, filled with spiritual power, I take you in my impure hands and pronounce over you the sacred words the universe was hiding and which you longed to hear:* "Hoc est enim corpus meum*: This is my Body.* Hic est sanguis meus. *This is my blood." And then I felt it: what was earth was transformed into Paradise, and what was human life was transformed into divine life. What was bread became God's body, and what was wine became sacred blood. Finally, Earth, with your sons and daughters, you came to God. You became God by participation. At home, at last.* (172)

Boff's book is well worth sustained attentiveness. It is a fierce wake-up call to the reality of God in whom we trust and to whom we respond; it is this God who will, in the end, not be mocked.

2

HOW THE MIGHTY HAVE FALLEN

I WAS BORN into a world of ecumenism. My church tradition, as far back as 1817 in Germany, was ecumenical. The Prussian Union, as it was called from its beginning, was a union of Reformed and Lutheran folk in Germany. The pastors of that tradition who came to the United States were termed *union men.* My church—the Evangelical and Reformed Church and then the United Church of Christ—has been persistently at the forefront of ecumenical ventures in the United States.

In my growing up years the most visible institutional form of ecumenism was the World Council of Churches, and I have followed it from early on through the years. I can only vaguely recall the First Assembly of the Council in 1948 in Amsterdam when I was thirteen. My dad subscribed to *The Christian Century* that I read early on, and which followed the Council closely. The Assembly was a daring meeting of reconciliation that brought together church leaders from opposing sides in World War II. Only later did I learn that my then to be father-in-law, Patrick D. Miller, had attended the Assembly on behalf of the Southern Presbyterian Church. The Assembly was governed and dominated by big-time church leaders, including the brave Swedish Lutheran archbishop, Nathan Soderblom. The meeting relied on the best academics and intellectuals that could be mustered, and Karl Barth was among its keynoters.

I have a much better memory of the Second Assembly in Evanston, Illinois in 1954. Because I was a college junior in Chicago, I could attend some of the sessions. I have two distinct memories of the Assembly. First, the opening service of the Assembly was a spectacle of a hundred thousand persons at Soldier Field. The many delegates to the Assembly processed into the stadium, all of them in ecclesial garb and the bright colors of their various cultures. We sang the great hymns of the church in rich and varied tongues and dialects, among them, "The Church's One Foundation." The spectacle was the public church that prospered in the 1950s at its most winsome and glorious. Second, I recall that in order to attend the substantive sessions of the Council one had to cross the picket lines of Carl McIntyre, the disgruntled, right-wing anti-Communist Presbyterian who charged the Council with being Communist. The third Assembly was held in New Delhi, India in 1961, indicating a decisive pull away from European domination of the Council, and a shift to the South and the East.

All of this I had in my memory as I happened upon *Wounded Visions: Unity, Justice, and Peace in the World Church after 1968* (2013) by Jonas Jonson, a retired Bishop of the Swedish Lutheran Church. Jonson considers the life and work of the World Council of Churches from the Fourth Assembly of the Council in Uppsala, Sweden in 1968 until the present. Jonson was among the Swedish bishops who had been vigorous participants in the work of the Council.

The 1960s were of course a time of turmoil in Western culture. It was in 1967 that Pope John XXIII convened the Second Vatican Council, an assembly that would dramatically bring the Roman Catholic Church more fully into contact with the realities of contemporary life. In 1966 there was an assembly in Geneva of the "Life and Work" component of the World Council that focused on "Church and Society." That remarkable meeting provided a series of books that were collections of papers from the Assembly that probed the implications of faith for current social reality. I remember that as a younger seminary teacher I read and reread those several books that contributed mightily to my education and my continuing slant on issues facing the church.

As Jonson sees, it was this Assembly of the World Council in Uppsala in 1968 that proved to be definitive for the future of the Council. In the previous Assemblies the accent had been more on the internal ordering of the church, and the reconciliation among the several churches after the war. Now in 1968, the Assembly turned outward toward the world and resolved that the world would determine the agenda for the issues to be faced in and by the church. In retrospect this was a turn toward secularization; Jonson identifies three decisive shifts in the church's center of gravity:

> from North to South;
> from a deductive to an inductive theological method, and
> from church ecumenism to secular ecumenism. (35)

From this point forward the Council gave its attention and energy to the crises facing the world, and sought to mobilize the resources of faith in order to make a generative response to those crises. To some great extent the Council was informed by the insistences of emerging "liberation theology," even as the Roman Catholic Church in Vatican II faced the same issues. The Council arrived, perhaps belatedly, at the conclusion that it did not need always to cast matters in the specific terms of gospel faith, but that the energy and purpose the gospel might be articulated in other ways that were not so explicitly and insistently *Christian*.

It is fair to say, I believe, that this Fourth Assembly was the high-water mark of the influence and prestige of the Council. The shift away from a Eurocentric base and a shift away from explicitly Christian subject matter served to portend the loss of energy and the engagement of important church leaders as they turned to more parochial matters in a time of church loss of members and dollars. In like manner these two shifts meant that the Council did not so readily draw the attention and participation of prominent academics who had immense authority on the issues under consideration. As a result the World Counsel became, in short order, more of a "people's movement" and much less top-down leadership from prestigious church leaders.

It is important to reckon with this redefinition and repositioning of the Council and its life and work. In order to underscore this crucial change, I have appealed to David's poetic pathos-filled lament over the deaths of King Saul and his beloved Jonathan at the hands of the Philistines. At the beginning and the end of his lament, David cries out:

> *How the mighty have fallen!* (2 Sam 1:19, 27)

The *mighty* in context refers to the king and his princely son. It is common among scholars to take David's lament as honest and without guile or pretense, even though these two deaths cleared the way for David's own anointment as king (2 Sam 2:1–7). The loss of Saul and Jonathan altered the landscape for Israel and for David, but it did not mean the end of Israel. Rather, these deaths cleared the way for new leadership in Israel.

In like manner, I suggest, in the World Council of Churches we have witnessed the dramatic departure from its life and work of big-time church leaders and big-time academics and intellectuals, so that the life and work of the Council was now to be carried on by more "normal" church members and leaders who tended to have much less star power. The mighty have indeed fallen (departed), but the work goes on, carried by passionate church people who are well and deeply grounded in faith, and who love the world with wisdom, courage, and steadfastness. Whereas in earlier days the Council, notably in the Geneva conference of 1966, imagined that the church would resolve the problems of the world, the Council must now focus on more modest efforts that are appropriate to the church's more modest place in society.

From Jonson's suggestive study we may consider four accent points that can be pertinent to the actual practice of life in a Christian congregation.

The Lautenberg Agreement in Basel in 1973 was a dramatic step in reconciling and defining the relationship of Lutheran, Reformed, and Union churches in Europe. That conference produced the happy formula, "Unity in Reconciled Diversity." That statement, with considerable realism, acknowledged that there are difficult and well-defined hindrances to full agreement among the churches on long-standing hard issues. Given those nonnegotiable differences, however, the churches nonetheless share a common faith in Christ and can do important work together. That good word just now might pertain, for example, to the United Methodist Church that is sharply divided over the presence of gay persons in the church. Such division need not preclude missional cooperation.

Jonson characterizes the ecumenical movement as "an alternative movement" standing at the side of losers in the process of globalization (160). As the world determines the church's agenda, the great and forceful reality of globalization is the overriding socioeconomic and political reality among us. Globalization amounts to enormous leverage in the hands of the few that easily overrides national boundaries as well as human rights. It has the force to reduce individual human persons to dispensable statistics and throwaway items that are no longer useful in the production of wealth. The work of the church is to stand with and for and on behalf of the "losers." In doing so, the church is participating in the continuing ministry of Jesus who was steadfastly on the side of losers. Thus he gives answer to John's messianic question in this way:

> *Go and tell John what you have seen and heard: the blind receive their sight, the lame walk, the lepers are cleansed, the deaf hear, the dead are raised, the poor have good news brought to them.* (Luke 7:22)

In order to be faithful, the church, in its worship, teaching, and proclamation must strongly accent its "alternative" from the ground up that parts company with the assumptions and practices of dominant globalism.

The great fact of globalism is its systemic violence before which vulnerable populations are helpless. The church must order its life and mission as a counter to violence, and must speak out in resistance to every such form of violence from rapacious markets to police brutality, to the wholesale distortion of communities. The church's witness must not only speak out, but must conduct its own life in a way congruent with nonviolence.

Jonson concludes:

> *At the global level, there is an increasing recognition that the world's problems are not Christian problems requiring Christian answers, but human problems that must be addressed together by all human beings. We know today that whether it is the issue of justice, peace, human rights, or the destruction of the environment, we need to work across boundaries of religions, nations, and cultures. There are calls for global movements and for a "global ethic" that would govern our life together.* (164)

In its heyday the World Council acted as if there were "Christian solutions" to world problems. But now we know better. Thus the "secularization" of the church means that the church is not committed to imposing its parochial solutions on world problems, but must give itself to "human solutions" that move beyond our conventional faith categories. It occurs to me, as Jonson may imply, that this means an ecumenism that is prepared to be fully allied with other faith traditions—Judaism, Islam—in seeking human answers that are grounded in the best impulses of our common, shared human legacy. This is no time for parochial self-defense. It is time, rather, for the full utilization of our life, resources, and traditions that lie behind much of what we have treasured in parochial ways.

This summing up for our new context of mission is peculiarly appropriate to the life and work of a local congregation. The earlier Assemblies of the Council had proposed large-scale engagement with social problems. In more recent time the focus of Assemblies concerns welcome to and solidarity with the left-behind. This is indeed an issue to be addressed locally. There is, I assume, no community of faith where such welcome is not at work. The church, quite locally, can be engaged with the victims of such violence, and can be engaged in solidarity alongside others who share a passion and hope beyond predatory violence. Thus the more recent reality of the Council in its weakness can bring its vision and passion much closer to the actual life of faith communities. The capacity of local congregations to be resolvedly alternative requires attentiveness from the ground up—in worship, in preaching, in study, in fellowship, and in willing self-giving. To be alternative has been our mandate since Moses convened Sinai, or since Jesus called his first disciples. My anticipation is that there is no escape from such an alternative among those wearied and exhausted by the exhaustive requirements and relentless threats of the dominant economy. Who among us does not need a "neighbor?" Being a neighbor is indeed an alternative. You know:

> *"Which of these three, do you think, was a neighbor to the man who fell into the hands of the robbers?" he said, "The one who showed him mercy." Jesus said to him, "Go, and do likewise."* (Luke 10:37)

3

HUMANITY ERASED?

THE JANUARY/FEBRUARY 2023 issue of *The Atlantic* offered an article by Adam Kirsch, "The End of Us." It is a reflection on current theory and speculation about "the end of humanity" as the culmination of the environmental crisis. The article reflects thought since the verdict of Michael Foucault that "Man could be erased, like a face drawn in the sand at the edge of the sea." The most helpful book I know on this hard subject is by my friend Timothy Beal, *When the Time is Short: Finding our Way in the Anthropocene* (2022).

Kirsch divides into two interpretive camps those who anticipate, and to some extent welcome, the erasure of humanity. On the one hand, there is "Anthropocene anti-humanism" that sees that humanity has engaged in self-destruction by the exploitation of creation. Humanity has used up and exhausted planetary resources, and now has brought upon itself the failure of human extravagance. This perspective believes that humanity is beyond rescue, and that its destruction is its deserved outcome for its unrestrained self-serving action. There is, in this perspective, no hope or possibility for the saving of the human project.

On the other hand, there is "transhumanism" that shares the view that the present ordering of life is beyond rescue or recall. This perspective has transcendent confidence in scientific and technological capacity and the reliance upon reason. It believes that given sufficient time, human rationality can devise new forms of possible life that are not limited to the destructive propensities of present practices. There is in this perspective a kind of "Dr. Strangelovian" seduction that strikes me as highly promethean. In the end this view shares with

"Anthropocene anti-humanism" a deep pessimism concerning any positive prospect for the present human enterprise. Both views foresee the inevitable termination of the present human project, the Anthropocene, that has imagined for a long time the mastery and domination of all creation by human wisdom and rationality.

These scientific speculations are well beyond my competence. But because the scientific, technological, and rational aspects of these carefully informed opinions spill over well beyond scientific, technological, and rational matters into more ultimate transrational questions, it seems fair and reasonable to try to see what linkages to the Anthropocene (and its failure and termination) might be made to the tradition of scripture. By way of a probe into these connections, in what follows I will consider a trajectory (in four parts) that probes the mystery and vocation of our human personhood. Two things are clear at the outset. First, all thought in scripture concerning human mystery and vocation is penultimate before the mystery of the holy God. Second, human mystery and vocation remain beyond decoding and explanation, and so invite continued probing. I will consider in turn four texts on the theme.

1. The first text is the familiar doxology of Psalm 8. We may note first of all that the psalm is framed in verses 1 and 9 by a grand doxology to YHWH who is acknowledged to be sovereign and majestic. Everything else in the psalm is subordinate to this grand claim. In verses 1b to 3 the psalmist probes the wonder of creation, its spectacular scope, and the capacity of the creator God to mobilize modest human folk to confound foes, enemies, and avengers.

Only in verse 4 does the Psalm come to the specificity of humanity. And when the subject is mentioned, it is as a question. The parallelism of the verse requires careful attention. In the first line, the "man" is *'ish*, the male human player in all of its weakness. In the tightly linked parallel in the second line, mention is made of the son-of-man, here *'adam*, "man" in his generic nobility. This latter usage is likely a reference to Genesis 1:26–27 and thus includes "male and female" in their power. I assume that the interface in the parallelism of *'ish* and *'adam* is not to stress gender as much as it is to reference humanity in its *weakness* and in its *strength*, that is, in its insoluble riddle. This curious combination of *man-in-weakness/man-woman in strength* is a modest creaturely reality in the midst of the grandeur of all creation. The place occupied by humanity in creation is modest at best. That human creature, moreover, remains an unanswered question.

In verse 4, however, we get a great rhetorical reversal on which the psalm pivots. The conjunction that introduces verse 5 challenges the conclusion of verse 4: Yet! Given such a modest place in creation, YHWH has nonetheless crowned humanity to lack little from being gods. (In the Hebrew, all of that is said in one verb!) The second line of verse 5 has an inverted word order for the sake of accent:

> *Glory and honor . . . you have given him!*

The two nouns are uninflected and absolute. The verb "crown" is an active performance. Humanity (in weakness/in strength) is now fully acknowledged to rule over creation. The inventory of creatureliness that follows in verses 6 to 8 intends to be all-inclusive with the range of species that evokes the work of the creator in Genesis 1:

> *You have put all things under their feet,*
> *all sheep and oxen,*
> *and also the beasts of the field,*
> *the birds of the air, and the fish of the sea,*
> *whatever passes along the paths of the sea.* (Ps 8:6–8)

Humanity is given governance, dominion, and control. The matter is a wonder because the psalmist (and Israel) knows about humanity in its feebleness. These verses do indeed sound like the Anthropocene. And so it would be except for the doxological framing of verses 1 and 9. Given that framing doxology, human domination is clearly penultimate. The creator God has not abdicated or abandoned sovereignty. Every move of governance by the human agent is responsive to and subject to divine governance that has not been revoked. It is doxology that precludes any would-be Anthropocene. When doxology and its practice of awe, wonder, and praise are abandoned, we will get the Anthropocene.

2. The well-known question of Psalm 8:4 is reiterated in Psalm 144. This Psalm begins in verses 1 and 2 with a statement of complete confidence in and reliance upon YHWH, the rock. These verses are dominated by the first-person pronoun, "my":

> *My rock,*
> *my hands,*
> *my fingers,*
> *my rock,*
> *my fortress,*
> *my stronghold,*
> *my deliverer,*
> *my shield.*

The one who speaks (David) is a mighty warrior who provides a full commentary on what it means to be strong and effective. All of that, however, is here recognized as derivative from the reality of God. In this assertion of self, there is full acknowledgment of penultimacy.

Our point of interest occurs in verse 3. The terms of Psalm 8 are reiterated, this time in reverse order, first *human beings in power* (*'adam*), and then *in weakness* (*'ish*). Again the psalm is in awe that this great creator God could know and think about humanity at all. The psalmist, even the great warrior, recognizes that human agents are like a passing breath or vapor that has no staying power at all. The psalm does not linger over the question, but moves on promptly to address God in petition (v. 5). The "ask" is for a theophany not unlike that of Sinai (vv. 5–6). Or alternatively, it is a bid to be saved from social troubles (vv. 7–8). The speaker places self in complete dependence upon YHWH, the rock.

The "new song" of verse 9 is a fresh doxology to God. It acknowledges YHWH as a God who rescues kings (who cannot rescue themselves) (v. 10). And then the psalmist prays for rescue (v. 11). The one who speaks presents themself as one who cannot do for self what needs to be done. This is the posture of a king who in helplessness is not adequate to the crisis to be faced.

And finally, in verses 12 to 15, there is a sweeping wish (petition!) for all the blessings of creation that only the creator God can give. It is a prayer that recognizes and gladly acknowledges creaturely dependence upon the creator. In sum, we can see that the momentary glance at humanity in verses 3 and 4 scarcely disputes the need for and the wonder of God. The human enterprise is fully submitted to the wonder of the creator God. Thus the framing doxology of Psalm 8:1 and 9 is here even more decisive. The human enterprise is fully enveloped in awe before God in a way that encompasses both human wonder and human need.

3. A third usage of our presenting question occurs in the speech of Job (Job 7:11–21). Job resolves to speak honestly, fully, and openly of all that vexes him so deeply (v. 11). In verse 12 his question indicates that God's surveillance of him is overstated and overwrought. He is weary of being monitored and supervised. His sleep is restless (vv. 13–14). He wants only to be left alone in his exhaustion, left alone that he may die (vv. 15–16). In verse 17 we have yet another version of our defining question:

> *What are human beings, that you make so much of them,*
> *that you set your mind on them?*

Here we have only one term for humanity, *'ish, human persons in frailty*. But the "man in frailty" is excessively supervised (*gdl*) by the creator God. God makes humanity too much of a subject of attention, causes him to be monitored too much. Job wants to escape such divine attention that seems to expect too much of him.

In verses 19 to 21 Job prays to be left alone, to be disregarded by the creator God, so that he may live his life in neglected obscurity. The divine gaze expects too much, monitoring every time he swallows his own spit, maybe every time he inhales or exhales. God is a "watcher of humanity," and no one can bear to be under such constant surveillance. It is enough that Job can wish his own death, or his non-being. It is the only way he knows to escape the daily review of his life as God's creature. Note well: there is nothing here of human splendor or grandeur, no thought of a governing Anthropocene. Thus the doxological splendor of Psalm 8 and the needy petition of Psalm 144 have settled into resentful compliance. Who wants to be the "creature in God's image" anyway? Certainly not Job; certainly not anyone who knows God's presence as a supervisory scorekeeper. Perhaps Job has misjudged God and misconstrued himself. Even so, this is a moment in the ongoing mystery of human personhood. Job speaks for all those who know that they cannot measure up to the expectations imposed by the creation itself and, by inference, by the creator God who keeps creation under daily review. At best this is a failed Anthropocene!

4. Finally we come to a fourth usage of our question, one that comes to us as a surprise. In articulating a weighty, priestly Christology, the writer of Hebrews 2:6–8 quotes Psalm 8:

> *What are human beings that you are mindful of them,*
> *or mortals, that you care for them?*
> *You have made them for a little while lower than angels;*
> *you have crowned them with glory and honor,*
> *subjecting all things under their feet.*

The Greek has a double use of *anthropos* that can translate *'adam* or *'ish* or both. There are two matters of note in these lines. In the parallel line, the Greek inserts a definite article before "son of man." The effect of this article is to make the given phrase "son of man" into a specific reference to Christ as "The Son of Man." Second, the NRSV neglects the point and translates the parallel line as "mortals." Thus in translation the specificity of the Greek is disregarded. The reference is then followed in the epistle with an anticipation that this "Son of Man" will face "suffering and death" and "face death for everyone" (v. 9). Thus the poetic lines of the psalm are refined as a declaration of the death of Jesus, and then the resurrection of Jesus who is "now crowned in glory and honor." The writer, moreover, concludes that God left nothing outside their control, even if that subjection is not yet seen everywhere.

When we consider this four-fold usage of the same phrasing, we can see that its claim is a poor offer for the production of the Anthropocene. In Psalm 8, the generous recognition of "man/son of man" is situated amid grand doxologies to God in verses 1 and 9. In Psalm 144 the formula concerning "man/son of man" is a bare mention in a poem that celebrates YHWH, the Rock, praises God with "a new song," and prays to God concerning the resources necessary for life. In Job 7:17, we have the weak man (*'enosh)*, without any parallel, with a death wish because God is too much surveillance for the living of his life. And in Hebrews 2, the "man/son of man" faces suffering and death. In none of these texts is there a masterful Anthropocene. In every case, the reality of the *anthropos* is as penultimate to the reality of God who is variously celebrated (Psalm 8), seen as essential for life (Psalm 144), hard to bear (Job 7), and entrusted to the son who must suffer and die. It should be evident enough that this textual trajectory offers a decisive alternative to any venture of Anthropocene governance, whether that governance is welcomed or repelled. It belongs to the communities of faith that are responsive to this textual tradition to resist and refuse any reduction of lived reality to the promotion of the Anthropocene age.

Having found in scripture a resolved alternative to Anthropocene reductionism, we may consider in turn the claims of *Anthropocene anti-humanism* and *transhumanism* amid the vistas of scripture. It seems obvious enough that Anthropocene anti-humanism can be readily and deeply linked to the Deuteronomic conviction that blessing comes to the obedient, and curse comes upon the disobedient. Anthropocene anti-humanism is the claim that it is the practice and policy of humanity that is resulting in the destruction of the natural environment. Thus humanity has acted in ways that evoke the destructive curse that is structural to created reality and that is the response of the creator God to such conduct. The simple calculus of Deuteronomy is unambiguous:

> *See, I have set before you today life and prosperity, death and adversity . . . Choose life so that you and your descendants may live.* (Deut 30:15,19)

See also the recital of curses in Deuteronomy 27:15–26, and the fuller recital of blessings and curses in Deuteronomy 28:1–68. The creator God presides over the processes of blessing and curse, but their implementation is intrinsic to creation itself. The matter is put succinctly by Hosea:

> *Swearing, lying, and murder,*
> *and stealing and adultery break out;*
> *bloodshed follows bloodshed.*
> *Therefore the land mourns,*
> *and all who live in it languish;*
> *together with the wild animals*
> *and the birds of the air,*
> *even the fish of the sea are perishing.* (Hos 4:2–3)

Disobedience causes nothing less than the shriveling of the earth in drought!

Perhaps the fullest, most direct articulation of this process wherein disobedience leads to destruction is in the wondrously symmetrical poem of Jeremiah:

> *I looked on the earth, and lo, it was waste and void,*
> *and to the heavens, and they had no light.*
> *I looked on the mountains, and lo, they were quaking,*
> *and all the hills moved to and fro.*
> *I looked, and lo, there was no one at all,*
> *and all the birds of the air had fled.*
> *I looked, and lo, the fruitful land was a desert,*
> *and all its cities were laid in ruins*
> *before the Lord, before his fierce anger.* (Jer 4:23–26)

These lines are commonly seen as a deliberate counterpoint to the creation liturgy of Genesis 1. Thus the creation is step-by-step dismantled in response to the unbearable conduct of Israel. That is, the practice of this community in contradiction to the creator will bring an end to God's life-giving creative order. No Anthropocene anti-humanism could make a claim stronger than this! That leaves us to ponder the caveat of verse 27:

> *Yet, I will not make a full end.*

From the mouth of the creator, not a full end! Is this verse only a pastoral softening of the harshness that precedes it? Is it wishful thinking of the faith community? Or is it a last minute reserve of the creator? We do not know; but it may give us pause.

It is not as obvious to me how *transhumanism* may be linked to scripture. I suggest that we may find a linkage between scripture and transhumanism in the way in which wisdom thinking in ancient Israel evolved into apocalyptic thought and writing. Almost alone, Gerhard von Rad has insisted that apocalyptic thought emerged from wisdom teaching and speculation. Von Rad's thought is that it was in wisdom that Israel developed an awareness of manageable, identifiable "ages" that are distinct and follow in sequence. That is, the wise were those who knew what time it was. Thus we are able to discern a real "end" to a historical period. We may see this succession of "ages" in the dream recital of Nebuchadnezzar (Dan 2:31–45). Von Rad cites the wisdom reflection of Ben Sirach as a case in point:

> *Rule over the world lies in the hands of God,*
> *and he sets over it the right man for the time.*
> *Power passes from one nation to another,*
> *because of arrogant acts of violence.* (10:4, 8)

Then Von Rad comments:

> *Of absolutely central significance for apocalyptic is the looking to an end to the present course of events, to a judgment and the dawning of a time of salvation, that is, its thoroughgoing eschatological orientation. (von Rad,* Wisdom in Israel, 278*)*

Just so, transhumanism concludes:

> *It believes that the only way forward for humanity is to create new forms of intelligent life that will no longer be Homo sapiens. Some transhumanists believe that genetic engineering and nanotechnology will allow us to alter our brains and bodies so profoundly that we will escape human limitations such as mortality and confinement to a physical body. Others await, with hope or trepidation, the invention of artificial intelligence superior to our own.* (Kirsch, "The End of Us," 60)

While we may readily take transhumanistic confidence in rationality and technology as a form of Promethean pride, we may also see it as the bold work of the wise in anticipation and reception of what is to come next, namely, an alternative life that is not dependent upon present human fragility. Such thinking at least has the virtue of being fully distinctive from what has gone before and failed, a distinctiveness that the sapiential apocalypticists of old would have welcomed.

I conclude my comment on this remarkable reflection on the Anthropocene age and its ending by Adam Kirsch by focusing on his conclusion. Kirsch observes that both of these trajectories of human destiny, Anthropocene anti-humanism and transhumanism, share a conviction:

> *The revolt against humanity has a great future ahead of it because it appeals to people who are at once committed to science and reason and yet yearn for the clarity and purpose of an absolute moral imperative.* (65)

And then this:

> *[This revolt] says we that we can move the planet, maybe even the universe, in the direction of the good, on one condition—that we forfeit our life meaning by giving it up.* (65)

This is a strong and unexpected echo of words that are most familiar to us in the gospel narrative:

> *For those who want to save their life will lose it, and those who will lose their life for my sake will find it.* (Matt 16:25)

Kirsch's final paragraph is stunning:

> *But both call for drastic forms of human self-limitation—whether that means the destruction of civilization, the renunciation of child-bearing, or the replacement of human*

> *beings by machines. These sacrifices are ways of expressing high ethical ambitions that find no scope in our ordinary hedonistic lives; compassion for suffering nature, hope for cosmic dominion, love of knowledge. This essential similarity between anti-humanists and transhumanists means that they may often find themselves on the same side in the political and social struggles to come.* (65)

The capacity for self-limitation is important. Kirsch refers to "our ordinary, hedonistic lives." But our "ordinary lives" do not need to be hedonistic, and for many people are not hedonistic. This accent on *compassion* for suffering nature, *hope* for cosmic dominion, and *love* of knowledge are all welcome. Thus believers in the gospel may go a long way with such a sentiment and summons. What are lacking here to which we pay attention as well are the elemental mandates of the gospel to love God and love neighbor. Thus transhumanists do not have God in their calculus, and do not regard the neighbor as a defining feature of our common life. We may indeed embrace Kirsch's mandate to *compassion*, but extend it to suffering humanity. We may be glad to *hope* with him for cosmic dominion, but recognize that sustainable dominion requires the emptying of self-regard. We may share his *love* of knowledge, but we know that our true love is not knowledge, but God and neighbor.

It may be that we face the erasure of the human. But an ethic more radical and more demanding than that of Kirsch may matter decisively. This is not the first time a community with a radical, demanding ethic has gone beyond our best rationality to deep risk. Our rationality, submitted to the cost of discipleship, in policy and in practice, is to refuse and resist human erasures one at a time, or all of us together. This is not an invitation to obscurantism or a denial of reality. Rather, it is an assertion that created reality is pliable and open to amendment. Such amendment may amount to nothing less than yielding of ourselves for the sake of creation, its creatures including its human creatures. We remain before the tricky question, What is a woman or man? What is humanity? The answer we give to that question is that we humans are "lord of all, servant of all." I suspect that Kirsch and his company would and could to some great extent share that conviction. The hard part is living it out, and thereby creating futures that are beyond technological rationality. That hard work is the reason we gather regularly around the news of dying and being raised to new life.

4

IN PRAISE OF THICKNESS

I WAS FIRST introduced, as were many of us, to "thickness" as an interpretive category by George Lindbeck's *The Nature of Doctrine: Religion and Theology in a Postliberal Age* (1984). Lindbeck writes:

> *Meaning is more fully intratextual in semiotic systems (composed, as they entirely are, of interpretive and communicative signs, symbols, and actions) than in other forms of ruled human behavior such as carpentry or transportation systems; but among semiotic systems, intratextuality (though still in an extended sense) is greatest in natural languages, cultures and religions which (unlike mathematics, for example), are potentially all-embracing and possess the property of reflexivity.* (114)

This heavy jargon-loaded statement is illuminated by his further commentary:

> *Only by detailed "familiarity with the imaginative universe in which . . . acts are signs" can one diagnose or specify the meaning of these acts for adherents of a religion. What the theologian needs to explicate "is a multiplicity of complex conceptual structures, many of them superimposed or knotted to one another, which are at once strange, irregular, and inexplicit, and which he must contrive somehow first to grasp and then to render." In rendering the salient features, the essential task "is not to codify abstract regularities, but*

> *to make thick description possible, not to generalize across cases but to generalize within them . . . There is, indeed, no more demanding exercise of the inventive and imaginative powers than to explore how a language, culture, or religion may be employed to give meaning to new domains of thought, reality, and action. Theological description can be a highly constructive enterprise.* (115)

Lindbeck has taken over the notion of "thick description" from Clifford Geertz (*The Interpretation of Cultures*, 1973) who came to understand that cultures are complex systems of signs, so that Lindbeck could see that religions as well are constituted by complex systems of signs. As a result, they require interpretation, and allow for great freedom in the exercise of imagination. They cannot be read simplistically off the surface, but require attentiveness to complexity, obscurity, and ambiguity.

With that awareness in the background, I read *Rules: A Short History of What We Live By* (2022) by Lorraine Daston. Her exposition of "rules" concerns the way in which a society is governed that includes both *thick* rules and *thin* rules. Of thin rules Daston avers:

> *[They] aspire to be self-sufficient and explicit. In principle, they wear their interpretations on their sleeves; they eschew commentary and have no need of hermeneutics. Nor must they enlist discretion to distinguish among cases and adjust to particular circumstances. Their generality presupposes that the class of cases to which they apply is unambiguous, that all cases in this class are identical, and that they will remain so for all eternity. Thin rules need not be concise—computer programs can go on for pages; ditto arithmetic calculations—but they cannot be vague.* (93)

It is most telling to notice her judgment that such rules require neither commentary nor hermeneutic. They are fully understood at first glance and leave no room for slippage.

By contrast, Daston's understanding of "thick rules" is that they require "discretion," both in terms of cognitive discretion in order to understand the norms and executive discretion in obedience or implementation. Thick rules, without that double discretion, are unhelpful and non-functional. Daston sees, moreover, that such thick rules are not themselves flat imperatives, but are rather models or paradigms for "patterns" of conduct, behavior, and policy.

The Bible, of course, is a collage of many rules. It is important, in the Bible as in our society, to distinguish between *thick rules* and *thin rules*. With a glance at the old distinction between "apodictic" and "casuistic" law enunciated by Albrecht Alt, it is useful to recognize that the baseline of scriptural rules, the Ten Commandments, is a set of "thick rules." That is, they set forth quite general norms for acceptable conduct in the covenant community; but quite clearly they require much interpretive work. Thus for example, the sixth commandment on "killing" has required a delicate distinction between murder and the legitimacy of war. We have gone to great lengths to parse the fourth commandment on sabbath in order to determine what constitutes "work" that would violate sabbath. The interpretive work on these commandments is endless in the communities said to be governed by the Decalogue. Both Jews and Christians have devoted great and continuing energy to the task. And while we may continue to quibble, there is no doubt that the Decalogue in sum intends *a neighborly community of security and well-being amenable to holiness of God* that precludes all other absolutes. As a consequence we are able to see that our variously proposed absolutes are inescapably penultimate, and our preferred certitudes are kept open and are, it turns out, much less than certain.

But the Bible also offers prominent examples of *thin rules* that voice quite specific requirements and leave nothing to imagination or interpretation. Thus, for example, the list of polluting foods in Deuteronomy 14:3–21 is unambiguous. The list neither requires nor permits interpretation or exposition. (We may however notice that in verse 21 it is as though Moses adds a qualifying thought about the disposal of such "unclean" animals, either by *giving* to "sojourners" or by *selling* to "foreigners." The latter options serve to protect the holiness of the people of God). While the intent of Isaiah 28:10, 13 is not completely clear, it may be cited as an example of the way in which the community may endlessly multiply more and more rules to cover more cases, until the catalogue of rules seems endless and inexhaustible:

For it is precept upon precept, precept upon precept,
line upon line, line upon line,
here a little, there a little . . .
Therefore the word of the Lord will be to them,
"Precept upon precept, precept upon precept,
line upon line, line upon line,
here a little, there a little."

The Hebrew is even more strikingly dramatic in its mesmerizing repetition:

ki zau lezau zau lzau
qau lqau qau laqau
ze'er sham ze'er sham.

The lines that sound like a ridiculing chant are reiterated in verse 13. The context suggests that this endless multiplication of rules is the work of a community that is in an anxious stance of self-destruction.

Thus we are able to see (along with many other evidences that could be cited) that Israel was capable of both *thick rules* and *thin rules*. We may hypothesize that in its times of greater anxiety or threat, Israel moved toward thinner rules that sought to eliminate ambiguity or uncertainty.

Daston judges that, starting in the seventeenth century, we can witness "the rise of more ambitious and less accommodating rules":

More ambitious, because they aimed to regulate either in greater detail . . . or to broaden their jurisdiction across

> *space and time. . . . Less accommodating, because either more explicit . . . or less open to discretion. . . . Increasingly, rules come shorn of the woolly coat of examples, exceptions, and appeals to experience that had cushioned earlier rules . . . against collision with unforeseen circumstances. Their tone becomes preemptory rather than expansive. In principle, these rules were expected to be obeyed to the letter; in practice, letter and spirit inevitably clashed in application to hard cases.* (241)

It may be that such a trajectory is reflective of the rise of science with René Descartes and Francis Bacon, and so an attempt to shape religious ethics according to scientific models. Or perhaps the move reflects anxiety about the collapse of the long-trusted heliocentric universe that was contradicted by Descartes and then by Galileo. Either way, the modern era is tempted to endless refinement of rules that eliminates interpretive alternatives and that refuses the playful freedom of interpretation. Daston notices as well that rules require exceptions:

> *Rules formulated to guide practice in situations in which the unexpected is the expected, whether in running a monastery or besieging a city, build in examples and exceptions . . . These thick rules are prepared to deal with any and all eventualities. Rules formulated for more stable, standardized circumstances, whether applying an algorithm to a routine calculation or setting speed limits for city streets, barely mention exceptions. Such would-be thin rules flourish in the same settings that averages do: where what happened in the past is a reliable guide to what will happen in the present and future. . . . An immense amount of infrastructure, both human and material, goes into making the world safe for thin rules. Workflows for calculations; sidewalks and broad, straight streets for city traffic; schooling and sanctions for everyone. Even under the most propitious circumstances, in*

> *which rules are so effectively drilled into schoolchildren that a slight change can provoke a national wave of protest, as in the case of orthography, rules must be constantly shored up by the editor's red pencil and the demon spellchecker. The court to equity in English law . . . or the dictionary of the Acadamie francaise . . . both venerable institutions established to adjudicate between rules and exceptions, offer eloquent testimony to the fact that exceptions we shall always have with us.* (269)

Of course it is the same in scripture. Thus for example, Leviticus 27:1–8 provides a catalogue of the "worth" of human beings, depending upon age. The catalogue is complete and precise. In verse 8, however, it is recognized that exceptions must be made to the precise catalogue for those "who cannot afford the equivalent." In such instances, the payment is to be determined by the decision of the priest who has freedom to make great allowances in particular transactions. Or in Deuteronomy 14:22–29, the rule requires regular offerings (tithes) to be taken to the place chosen by YHWH. But then in verses 24 and 25, an exception is made if the place of YHWH's choosing is far away:

> *But if, when the Lord your God has blessed you, the distance is so great that you are unable to transport it, because the place where the Lord your God will choose to set his name is too far away from you, then you may turn it into money. With the money secure in hand, go to the place that the Lord your God will choose.* (Deut 14:24–25)

The exception reflects the realism of the rule makers.

We are able to see the same contrast of thick and thin rules in the New Testament. In the long polemic of Matthew 23:13–36 we can see the critique of a phony sacerdotal system that has endless requirements:

> *Woe to you, scribes and Pharisees, hypocrites! For you tithe mint, dill, and cummin, and have neglected the weightier matters of the law: justice and mercy and faith.* (Matt 23:23)

The managers of the dominant system had devised extensive rules for tithing, not unlike Deuteronomy 14:22–29. These were apparently rules for the "taxation" of every commodity, right down to the most minute spice. (Such specificity is perhaps nicely echoed in the intense exactitude of the US Federal Tax Code.) That exactitude, however, had "blinded" the leadership to the large realities of covenantal faith (see Matt 23:16). This exactitude, moreover, was a distraction that caused neglect of what really matters to a Torah-keeping community. By contrast, consider the neighborly practice of the church commended by the apostle Paul. His catalogue is "by contrast" to the self-indulgence of Galatians 5:19–21, but is also "by contrast" to religious punctiliousness:

> *By contrast, the fruit of the Spirit is love, joy, peace, patience, kindness, generosity, faithfulness, gentleness, and self-control.* (Gal 5:22–23)

This list of positive practices lacks precision but offers general categories that are to be acted out with specificity among the faithful. Paul's conclusion, "There is no law against such things," is a recognition that he is not articulating a "law," but rather a model of conduct that can guide the community in a most generalized way. At the same time, we can easily recognize that this list of attitudes is readily available to live out in specific practice, even while we "negotiate" the radicality of the exposition.

In my reflection on this suggestive discussion by Daston, my thinking has gone like this:

1. *Good (thick) rules leave much hard work to do.* Like the Decalogue or the catalogue of Paul, matters are not specified. We must each time do the hard interpretive work of deciding how, in what way, and

to what extent we will "obey" this rule. On the one hand, this means that the congregation that claims the text of scripture must be engaged in the active, knowing, critical work of moral reflection. While there was a time when such an ethic was more or less in the woodwork of our society and could be taken for granted, it is no longer so. And so the church and its pastors must be engaged in probing the ways in which the "thick rules" of our faith pertain to every sphere of our common life. On the other hand, it is inescapable that such hard, serious work, interpretive work—that will be filtered through our fears, our hopes, and our vested interests—is sure to be quarrelsome and contentious. Indeed a community that is seriously engaged in such moral reflection is sure to be a community of contestation. (To some great extent we have avoided this hard work by self-selection into homogeneous communities, on which see *The Big Sort: Why the Clustering of Like-Minded Americans is Tearing Us Apart* [2009] by Bill Bishop).

2. It seems clear enough that *we have continued the trajectory that Daston notes in the seventeenth century to embrace thin rules*. Thus in our "age of anxiety" there is a great hunger for certitude that will serve to fend off the seeming chaos. It is easy enough to observe this propensity in right-wing reductionism, perhaps its most extreme form represented by Florida Governor Ron DeSantis in his passion for specific rules of exclusion. Such thin rules function to banish any ambiguity and to make matters singularly clear in terms of social expectations and requirements. Liberals also have an inclination to reduce the thick rules of the gospel to specific requirements about inclusion and social justice, so that anyone who thinks otherwise is dismissed or disregarded. Every time there is such a reduction, either liberal or conservative, it is an attempt to control the interpretive narrative and to dominate moral discussions that are never without a dimension of ambiguity. In the end, there cannot be enough thin rules, conservative or liberal, to eliminate the need for adjudication and conversation in the community.

3. *After all our thin rules, we do not live our lives by such rules.* Rather, we rely on matters of relational trust. Thus even the Decalogue is introduced by reference to the emancipatory God of the exodus. The

Decalogue is simply a model for how to live well in response to that faithful emancipatory God. Thus the rules are guidelines for relationship. It is for that reason that even the most zealous rule-enforcers in the community—whether liberal or conservative—can still be moved to compassion and generosity by the needy plight of a neighbor. It is a core claim of this moral community that in the end we do not live *by rules* but *by relationships*. Thus, "the sabbath was made for humankind, and not humankind for the sabbath" (Mark 2:27). It is for a compelling reason that Jesus, in the manner of the rabbis, was able to see that the commandments—rules sweepingly thick or rules particularly thin—are finally about true love—love of God and love of neighbor (Mark 12:28–34). Our most treasured thick rules are about how to act out those two true loves.

We in the church might take a deep breath in order to recognize that we are a rule-trusting, rule-making, rule-obeying community. But all of our trusting, making, and obeying of rules is in the service of our two true loves. And when our anxieties de-center that truth in our lives, we may twitter away our energy on rules that are designed precisely to maintain our control and fend off chaos. Too much of the time we want to escape the hard, contested work of interpretation. But love requires it. Indeed, interpretation is an ongoing exploration of how we live out the two loves that define our lives. Daston sees that our rules are prophetic and aspirational. Thus those who formulate rules envision

> *an order that did not yet exist and perhaps never would: a fashion for unchanging simplicity and restraint in dress, a city where the houses were all neatly numbered and it was safe to cross the street; a nation united by a language spoken and spelled by all citizens in the same way. There was a utopian element in these hard-headed regulations.* (209)

Amid the thick rules of our faith, we are invited to a concrete yearning for the coming rule of God where the last are first, and the humble are exalted.

5

JUSTICE IN THE GATE

THE PRESENT US Supreme Court is on the loose with its pernicious enterprise of so-called originalism. The inescapable outcome of its brand of "originalism" is that eventually the only members of our society whose rights are secure are white male property owners. They are the only ones in the purview of the "original" constitution. The present court is on its way in that direction without any check or restraint, with its capacity to run roughshod over the executive and legislative branches of government. That court, moreover, has not arisen by accident, but by the careful engineering of those who would secure rights for the monopoly of white male property owners at the expense of all others.

Of course the question concerning the court is one of jurisprudence, constitutional law, and our several trajectories of interpretation of the constitution. The recognition that the issue requires expertise in jurisprudence, however, does not mean that the Christian community must remain mute concerning the crisis evoked by the present court. In considering how the church might respond to this threat to our democratic society, I conclude that the church must bear witness from its scriptural text, and insist that *profound human interests* are at stake beyond the fine points of the law.

To that end I suggest that we turn to the best offer of the Bible concerning judicial matters, the book of Deuteronomy. Both Norbert Lohfink* and S. Dean McBride** have proposed that Deuteronomy

* 1 Norbert Lohfink, *Great Themes from the Old Testament* (T&T Clark, 1982).

** John T. Strong and Steven S. Tuell, eds., Constituting *Community: Studies in the Polity of Ancient Israel in Honor of S. Dean McBride* (Eisenbrauns, 2005).

offers something like a "constitution" for Israel with a guarantee of "separation of powers." Thus Moses in Deuteronomy authorizes judges (17:2–7), an appeals court (17:813), kings (17:14–20), priests (18:1–8), and prophets (18:15–22). All of these officials are in the service of maintaining a covenant community of neighbors.

Three texts in Deuteronomy in particular draw our attention.

1. *Deuteronomy 16:18–20* enunciates the deep and demanding norm of governance for a judicial system for a covenantal community:

> *You shall appoint judges and officials throughout your tribes, in all your towns that the Lord your God is giving you, and they shall render just decisions for the people. You must not distort justice; you must not show partiality; and you must not accept bribes, for a bribe blinds the eyes of the wise and subverts the cause of those who are in the right. Justice, and only justice, you shall pursue, so that you may live and occupy the land that the Lord your God is giving you.* (Deut 6:18–20)

It is telling indeed that in this terse provision, the single warning concerning judges is the *temptation for bribes* from moneyed people that skew decisions. This accent has poignant contemporaneity for us as we consider the huge "gifts" Justices Alito and Thomas have received from people or entities with interests in cases before the Court. One may wonder, as such bribes inescapably "blind the eyes" of judges. Beyond that, of course, everything depends upon the substance of "justice" that Moses will trace out in Deuteronomy.

2. In *Deuteronomy 17:2–7*, Moses authorizes a local judicial procedure, which of necessity depends upon judges to decide cases reliably. This provision concerns proper procedure including witnesses. The definitive concern here is idolatry; as we know (and Israel knew), however, false gods lead inescapably to false economics and false politics, thus a skewing of the neighborhood. Karl Marx put it succinctly:

> *The criticism of heaven is thus transformed into the criticism of earth,*
> *the criticism of religion into the criticism of law, and*
> *the criticism of theology into the criticism of politics.*
> *(David McLellan,* The Thought of Karl Marx: An Introduction, 22).

Judges are to guard against distortions of neighborliness via false gods, and so false economics and false politics.

3. The additional provision of *Deuteronomy 17:8–13* establishes a "court of appeal" for difficult cases. Of interest here is the verb *yrh* that we translate as "interpret." That is, appeals court judges are to "interpret justice" so that matters of guilt and innocence are not given through "fortune cookie" formulas but require wise adjudication and freedom in interpretation. We may thus imagine that the appeals court had, for Moses, great leeway in settling disputes according to the Torah filtered through wisdom. In this tradition such appeals judges are identified as Levitical priests, that is, the community of Torah teachers who are themselves responsible for the formulation of Deuteronomy. When we seek the substance of such court rulings based on covenantal Torah filtered through wisdom, we must look to the particulars of Torah provisions. We may notice four such provisions in the corpus of Deuteronomy, though there are many more:

- No interest charged on loans to Israelites (23:19–20)
- Respect for the poor by not taking their property as security for loans (24:10–13)
- Prompt payment of wages to the poor (24:14–15)
- Allowance for the poor to live on resources from land owned by others (24:19–22)

These several instances of case law suggest that the concern and tilt of the Torah and thus the mandate for local and appeal courts is restorative justice, whereby the vulnerable in the community are protected from the avarice of the strong. The protection of *the poor*, that is, those without advocates, is a primary function of the court.

We may notice the way in which prophetic utterances appeal to these Torah provisions for justice. In Amos 5 the prophet offers a series of five imperatives that build from "YHWH" to "justice":

> *seek me;*
> *seek the Lord;*
> *seek good;*
> *hate evil and love good;*
> *establish justice in the gate.* (Amos 5:4, 6, 14–15)

The rhetorical sequence makes clear that the practical substance of "YHWH" is justice of a restorative kind (see Jeremiah 22:15–16). Thus the village and tribal elders "held court" at the village gate. The prophet reminds them that their purpose is to ensure justice for the vulnerable. When we look for the claims of justice in the book of Amos, we can see that it concerns the poor who are cheated in the economy (8:4–6) by the advantaged who in their self-indulgence neglect the well-being of the community (6:1–7). Thus prophetic utterance appeals to the old covenantal norms that provide for the economic viability of the entire community, rich and poor. The matter of "hate the good and love the evil" (a reversal of Amos is sounded in Micah 3:2). The summons is to restorative justice for those who are maltreated in an economy of unrestrained greed.

The trick in the historical process of Israel was to transfer the *old covenantal priorities of Torah* into *the policy and practice of monarchy*. We do not have much data about this transference; attention, however, may be paid to 2 Chronicles 19:5–11. It is reported that King Jehoshaphat appointed judges, that is, he established a royal judiciary. He charged the judges:

> *Consider what you are doing, for you judge not on behalf of human beings but on the Lord's behalf; he is with you in giving judgment. Now, let the fear of the Lord be upon you;*

> *take care what you do, for there is no perversion of justice*
> *with the Lord your God, or partiality, or taking of bribes.*
> (vv. 6–7)

Again the provision is most specific about bribes! The general principle of this provision is that judges are to act on behalf of YHWH, the God of restorative justice. The justification of this provision is an echo of Moses in Deuteronomy and of Amos the prophet. It is recognized that such justice may be skewed; and what will most skew justice is the economic leverage of the wealthy, that is, bribery. This action by King Jehoshaphat is not reported in the account of his reign in 1 Kings 22:41–50, and we have no way of knowing of its historicity. I recall that in an early unpublished paper Patrick Miller took this report on Jehoshaphat as having some historical claim to it. In any case, this belated royal report imagines that royal courts in Israel could and must rule *in favor of the neighborhood*, which means *adjudication on behalf of the poor* in order to fend off the predatory passions of the wealthy.

While the historical evidence for transference from Moses to monarchy is not very strong or very specific, what we can see is the recurrence of the same accents in Torah, in prophetic urgency, and in belated historical reportage. All are agreed that the proper work of Israel is to establish a legal apparatus that faithfully reflects the will of YHWH in its protection of the vulnerable. There can be no doubt that this is the substantive insistence of scripture.

So now the church, along with the synagogue, has these texts on our hands. The texts linger in their insistence on attention. The church has these texts, moreover, in the midst of a judicial crisis in our society in which our Supreme Court has been fully captured by powerful interests that are strenuously anti-neighborly, and that intend to empower and authorize the worst predatory greed imaginable. Thus the so-called originalism of the present court inclines to protect and acknowledge the benefits of constitutional justice only for a select segment of the population, namely, white male property owners.

We cannot and must not be simplistic about the matter. It is neither possible nor wise simply to overlay biblical models on a pluralistic democratic society, even though some on the right want to do exactly that on other matters. We can be much more knowing than that simplification. The church surely does have standing ground in scripture to take a critical stance toward the Supreme Court, and to insist that the Court must give attention to the restorative justice that tells precisely against the advantaged interests of white male property owners. At a local level, the work of the church is likely not to make sharp direct engagement. Rather, the work is to teach the congregation about the centrality of restorative justice to our faith, with a recognition that such restorative justice requires concrete governmental engagement. This tradition insists that the courts have work to do as protectors of and advocates for the vulnerable who are without protector or advocate. In the Old Testament, the God of the covenant and the agents of that God become protectors of those who have no other male advocate. Thus the God of covenant is "the father of orphans" (Psalm 68:5) who summons the covenant community to be precisely such protectors.

It turns out that the royal liturgy enacted in the Jerusalem temple understood the royal responsibility for such restorative work. Thus the royal Psalm 72 was likely a part of that recurring Jerusalem liturgy, perhaps sung by the temple choirs:

Give the king your justice, O God,
and your righteousness to a king's son.
May he judge your people with righteousness,
and your poor with justice . . .
May he defend the cause of the poor of the people,
give deliverance to the needy,
and crush the oppressor . . .
For he delivers the needy when they call,
the poor and those who have no helper.

He has pity on the weak and the needy,
and saves the lives of the needy.
From oppression and violence he redeems their life;
and precious is their blood in his sight. (Ps 72:1–2, 4, 12–14)

The psalm is as clear and unambiguous as is the Torah and Amos. Indeed, the song goes on to indicate that it is precisely such restorative justice on the part of the royal house that can ensure the well-being and longevity of the king and the continuing dynasty:

May he live while the sun endures,
and as long as the moon,
throughout all generations.
May he be like rain that falls on the mown grass,
like showers that water the earth.
In his days may righteousness flourish
and peace abound, until the moon is no more.
May he have dominion from sea to sea,
and from the River to the ends of the earth.
May his foes bow down before him,
and his enemies lick the dust.
May the kings of Tarshish and of the isles render him tribute,
may the kings of Sheba and Seba bring gifts.
May all kings fall down before him,
all nations give him service. (Ps 72:5–11)

It is likely that the psalm was a staple of the royal liturgy in Jerusalem, recited and heard over and over and over. Indeed, the psalm and its summons may have become old hat (old crown!) for the king and his entourage. But sometimes, the old cadences of liturgy strike one as new, fresh, and challenging. Perhaps King Jehoshaphat one day noticed and actually heard the psalm. Maybe the psalm triggered the new judicial institutions of the king. In any case, King Jehoshaphat undertook a new enterprise that placed the old covenantal vision of Moses at the heart of his royal regime.

The work of the church in its liturgy is not unlike the ancient liturgy for the ancient king in Jerusalem. We sound the old cadences of restoration over and over. Once in a great while, the sounds of the liturgy summon and impact. Thus it may be that the church can be the "alert" for the public work of restorative justice in our society. Such an alert could summon and empower its mostly unsuspecting members to new awareness, new resolve, and new public possibility. It may be that the testimony of the psalm, the claim the Torah, and prophetic utterance, heard in concert, could evoke fresh critical awareness and new constructive energy. This critical awareness could permit us to see the systemic miscarriage of justice by the present Court. This new constructive energy might lead the congregation to insist on a different kind of public leadership. Theological legitimacy matters to our public institutions. The matter of the court is no exception. When the court forfeits its theological legitimacy, we may indeed declare that "the glory has departed." It could be otherwise! That is the hope for our common public life every time the church convenes.

Part II

STANDING AGAINST THE POWERS

6

MAPPING AS POWER

LAURA TRETHEWEY IS an environmental and ocean journalist. In *The Deepest Map: The High-Stakes Race to Chart the World's Oceans* (2023) she reports that she enlisted on a mapping cruise on the *Nautilus*. Her book proceeds in a chatty, informal way to give an account of her experiences and observations on board the *Nautilus*. Early on, she quotes the journalist, Stephen Hall:

> *A map always presages some form of exploitation.* (p. 5)

And indeed, her use of "high-stakes" in her title suggests that mapping the bottom of the oceans constitutes, among competitive nations, a chase of resources in the service of exploitation and domination.

Trethewey's sentence linking "mapping" and "exploitation" set me to thinking about maps that exhibit the power to exploit. Likely the most pernicious map in the Bible is the sketch of King Solomon's tax districts (1 Kgs 4:7–19). That map articulates twelve tax districts with twelve officers, each of which "had to make provision for one month of the year" (v. 7). Two factors suggest the urgency of these tax districts for the royal apparatus that ran roughshod over old tribal boundaries. First, among the tax officers are two of King Solomon's own sons-in-law, Binabinadab (v. 11) and Ahimaaz (v. 15). Their presence in the roster of tax officials suggests both how important tax collection was to the king, and how lucrative it was. Second, the index of luxurious foods at the king's table attests to how much revenue was required to finance the royal appetite (1 Kgs 4:22–23).

It is evident in the narrative of 1 Kings 12:1–19 that the mapping of royal tax districts imposed unbearably heavy tax burdens on the peasant subjects of the king, so heavy that resistance and rebellion were evoked among the populace. The outcome of the peasant action was the killing of the king's "taskmaster over forced labor" (v. 18) and the secession of ten tribes from the royal state. In effect, the resistant crowd tore up the map, and made Solomon's tax collection impossible.

On May 4, 1493, Pope Alexander VI issued a decree entitled Inter caetera that detailed a division of the Americas between the Kingdoms of Spain and Portugal, two states that were fully committed to papal authority. In effect the Pope mapped out the zones of conquest, exploitation, and wealth for the two European powers. Implicit in the decree is the assumption that white Europeans were free and entitled to claim, occupy, and possess the new world, its population, and its resources. While this division of the New World in this way was promptly challenged by England, France, and the Netherlands, the papal decree set in motion the rapacious contest for control of the rich land that was already otherwise inhabited. Thus the new papal mapping declared and legitimated new "ownership" of the new land, as though the pope and his white European subjects were fully entitled to it. The papal decree initiated the contest of colonialization that was to persist well into the twenty-first century.

These two mappings from long ago fully illustrate the Trethewey's thesis that *mapping* is for *exploitation*. Thus Solomon, via his tax districts, exploited his peasant subjects. Thus the papal decree authorized brutal exploitation of the new land, its population, and its resources. These two old maps set me to thinking about more contemporary mappings that unambiguously were designed for exploitation. I could think of three such practices that are so familiar to us that we may fail to notice their pernicious intent.

First, banks in the United States have for a very long time been engaged in *redlining*, a practice that intends and leads to discriminating home lending habits. The outcome of such mapping by banks is to deny loans to some areas and neighborhoods, while at the same time readily investing in others. Such mapping has helped to produce and sustain disadvantaged neighborhoods that are easily dismissed as "slums," that is, neighborhoods denied resources. The basis of such mapping has most often been related to race, so that banks could systematically deny loans to neighborhoods of non-white neighbors. The practice has been unofficial and covert, and for that reason has prevailed for a long time as though it were beyond challenge.

Second is the current vigorous contestation concerning maps for *voter registration and voting*. Some states, through legislative action, have been able to draw district lines in ways that disempower non-white voters, either by depleting their voting strength or by placing non-white voters in a few districts, thus leaving many more districts free from effective non-white voters. The Voting Rights Act of 1965 moved effectively against such racist gerrymandering. Since that time, however, the courts have, at every turn, sought to dismantle the force of the Voting Rights Act, leaving state officials free to map out racist discrimination.

Third, even in such local matters as *school districts*, mapping has been concerned with racist distinctions. Thus in my long-time hometown of Webster Groves, a suburb with a very small Black population, the school board reorganized the district in the 1960s and strategically placed three Junior High schools in the district that would channel Black students in the district into one school, so that the other two schools, located in wealthier parts of town, would remain free from Black students. (This is the same community that chose, for a while, to close its public swimming pool rather than to integrate it racially.)

In all these instances—*bank loans*, *voting districts*, and *school districts*—mapping was clearly designed for exploitative purposes. It is easy enough to imagine that in discussions that produced these maps the matter was regarded as "high-stakes," to take up Trethewey's phrase. In every case, the "victims" of such maps were largely rendered powerless and forced to accept assigned places and roles of vulnerability. Thus:

- In King Solomon's regime, the peasants were helpless, until they mobilized.
- In 1493 the native populations in the Americas were largely powerless against European force, even though there was resistance to such imposition.
- On redlining, such action was slowly challenged through legal action, but for a long time was assumed to be legitimate and left unchallenged.
- Concerning voting rights, the Act of 1965 mattered decisively, but the long process of dismantling the requirements of the law continues even now.
- In school segregation, the victims were largely powerless, with some indecision whether the urgency concerned integrated schools, or good schools that might remain segregated.

We can all remember the mapping of the Soviet Union over Eastern Europe. The maps were usually in red. And then on June 12, 1987, President Reagan in Berlin boldly addressed the Soviet Union: "Mr. Gorbachev, tear down that wall." He referred to the Berlin Wall, but the point was far larger than that. He might have said, "Tear up that map." Surely the president said more than he knew, because his demand was the endless demand everywhere of the vulnerable against the powerful who have imposed their will and order on the world.

Of course gospel faith has a stake in these matters and must mobilize all of its courage and insistence against such exploitative mapping, wherever it occurs. In a dramatic instance of such courage and insistence the leaders of the tribal peasants of Israel convened at Shechem (1 Kgs 12). Their intent was to dismantle or tear-up the power arrangements of Solomon's that provided royal opportunities for exploitation by the crown. In the horizon of the New Testament the great map drew lines of exclusion between Jews and gentiles. We may take these maps in Israel (Solomon's districts) and in the church (Jews and gentiles) as paradigmatic for all the mappings I have enumerated here, along with many others. Powerful people are always drawing maps of privilege, advantage, and exclusion.

In John 4:7–15 concerning "the Samaritan woman at the well," the narrative gives us background commentary:

> *Jews do not share things in common with Samaritans.*
> (John 4:9)

The matter is front and center in the narrative of Acts 10. Peter, good faithful Jew that he is, refuses the command of the voice of heaven, "Get up, kill, and eat." Peter has a clear mapping in his head and heart about the proper relationship between Jews and Samaritans.

> *By no means, Lord; for I have never eaten anything that is profane or unclean.* (Acts 10:14)

Against his resistance and refusal, the voice asserts:

> *What God has made clean, you must not call profane.*
> (Acts 10:15)

In effect that voice from "elsewhere" intends to delegitimate the long-standing map of Jewish-gentile relationships. The declaration of gentile food as "unclean" is characteristic of such mapping. The distinction between "clean" and "unclean" is long-running in the Bible (see Deut 14:3–20). In parallel fashion, racism in our culture easily has it that Blacks are "unclean" and smell badly, and therefore must be shunned and excluded. Indeed, we may see a belated reiteration of Peter's narrative in the lunch-counter sit-ins of the 1960s. The reason to "reserve the right to refuse service" to anyone was specifically a way to exclude Blacks from lunch counters. The daring sit-in protests were designed to destroy the maps of racist exclusion in our culture.

It turns out, in the New Testament church, that the division between Jews and gentiles in the community of faith was definitional for the map-destroying import of the gospel. The most programmatic statement of the rejection of such maps is in Galatians 3:8, likely an early baptismal formula:

> *There is no longer Jew or Greek, there is no longer slave or free, there is no longer male or female; for all of you are one in Christ Jesus.* (Gal 3:28)

Paul's declaration addressed three common barriers that defined social relationships in his world, and that continue to make the same divisions even among us:

- There was, as among us, a decisive division between *Greeks and Jews*;
- There was, as among us, a sharp distinction between *slaves and free people*, and we may add, among the descendants of slaves and owners among us.
- There was, as among us, a barrier between *males and females*, with males enjoying unspeakable privileges in a world with a pernicious maintenance of the "glass ceiling."

To this triad we may in our time, add a fourth such distinction between *heterosexuals* and *gays and lesbians*. And now, in Christ, no more! Because "in Jesus Christ" all such barriers are overcome. All such maps that trace out advantage and exclusion are now nullified in the gospel. Jesus Christ has put an end to the common ways in which we have apportioned the benefits of our common life. This assertion by Paul is reiterated in the later Epistle to the Ephesians:

> *For he is our peace; in his flesh he has made both groups into one and has broken down the dividing wall, that is, the hostility between us.* (Eph 2:14)

Our several maps trace out and legitimate walls that breed hostility. And now Christ Jesus has eliminated such distinctions, so that all parties have access to the resources for well-being.

As I was writing this comment I received a first copy of a new book authored by my friend, Troy Jackson, along with Chuck Mingo, *Living Undivided: Loving Courageously for Racial Healing and Justice* (2024). Jackson is a smart, fearless community organizer who has for a long, effective time faced the ways in which racism divides our society. The book grows out of the long experience of the authors of dealing with racism, and finding practical, immediate ways to overcome racist barriers in our society. In their final summation, these authors offer a summons:

> *This entire book has been written to encourage you to walk humbly, love mercy, and do justice. And to see that by doing so, God can use you in the work of racial healing and justice.*
>
> *It starts with you.*
> *It starts with you choosing courage over fear.*
> *It starts with you choosing love over indifference.*
> *It starts with you allowing God's redeeming power to lead you away from*
> *stagnancy toward loving action.* (225)

It belongs to the early church, as it belongs to the contemporary church, to be at work overcoming such barriers, that is, nullifying such maps that maintain and protect privilege and so require disadvantage for others. Trethewey regards the mapping of the bottom of the oceans as "high-stakes," a term in her subtitle. By that she means that the nations are rivals and must compete in order to control resources that are to be found in the oceans. National interest, as Trethewey understands, is always to seek to establish control, and therefore privilege and advantage. But the work of the gospel is to the contrary. In our own season of scarcity, fear, and greed prone to violence, we erect many barriers. The church, to the contrary, insists that such barriers, distinctions, and privileges should be and can be overcome. The God of love and justice engages, always again, in an embrace of creation that draws together all that we divide in fear and greed. That work is now urgent among us.

7

THE VOICE OF THE VICTIM

WHAT IF: OUR historical moment is not unlike that moment just before the flood?

Now the earth was corrupt in God's sight, and the earth was filled with violence (Gen 6:11).

The catalog of violence among us is obvious:

- the school shootings as some prefer their guns to our children
- our public rhetoric is now at the edge of violence, or beyond the edge
- our refusal to host desperate immigrants, so that they die in risky, courageous efforts at escape
- the wide-eyed violence of police brutality
- the unrestrained exploitation of creation, etc., etc., etc.

What if: our current calamities are not unlike that of the flood when Holy Hiddenness mandated the earth to deathliness?

> *And God said to Noah, "I have determined to make an end of all flesh, for the earth is filled with violence because of them; now I am going to destroy them along with the earth.* (Gen 6:13)

The flood story is not a winner. The ark should not be noticed in a positive way, but as a massive failure on the part of Holiness who could manage to save only one family and sparse representatives of other species.

The flood narrative is a paradigmatic tale that recurs concretely and historically in the life-work of Jeremiah. The prophet lived at a moment of the collapse of his social order, the failure of social institutions, and the abandonment of Israel by the God of Israel. Jeremiah was left to bring that reality to speech amid a society that much preferred denial. He gave voice to the violence that "official Jerusalem" wanted to disregard:

> *Also on your skirts is found*
> the lifeblood of the innocent poor,
> *though you did not catch them breaking in.*
> *Yet in spite of all these things you say,*
> *"I am innocent."* (Jer 2:34–35)

It was easy enough to spill the lifeblood of the innocent who are characteristically without protection or social leverage:

> Violence and destruction *are heard within her;*
> *sickness and wounds are ever before me.* (Jer 6:7)

> *If you do not oppress the alien, the orphan, and the widow, or shed innocent blood in this place, and if you do not go after other gods to your own hurt, then I will dwell with you in this place.* (Jer 7:6–7)

It is recurringly the "innocent blood" of the powerless that is the measure of corruption and violence:

> *For whenever I speak, I must cry out,*
> *I must shout,* "Violence and destruction*!"* (Jer 20:8)

Jeremiah is surrounded by conspiracy theorists, who whisper,

> *"Terror is all around!"* (Jer 20:10)

The prophet nonetheless can still imagine a reversal of that dismaying practice:

> *Act with justice and righteousness, and deliver from the hand of the oppressor anyone who has been robbed. And do no wrong or violence to the alien, the orphan, the widow, or* shed innocent blood *in this place.* (Jer 22:3)

The single remedy to such systemic violence is simply a determined resolve for "righteousness and justice" that refuses violence to the powerless, and that would not shed innocent blood. Jeremiah sees his social reality clearly, without distraction by any distorting ideology; he also sees the demanding path to an alternative, namely, the valuing of the powerless.

I have been led to these reflections on social systemic violence by reading *Truth and Repair: How Trauma Survivors Envision Justice* (2023) by Judith Herman. Herman is already known among us for her conversation-changing book, *Trauma and Recovery: The Aftermath of Violence—From Domestic Abuse to Political Terror* (1992). In that book she introduced us to a study of "trauma" that has impacted the study of the books of Jeremiah and Ezekiel. See Juliana Claassens, "Jeremiah: The Traumatized Prophet" (2021), Ruth Poser, "Ezekiel as Trauma Literature," (2020) and Refael Furman, "Trauma and Post-Trauma in the Book of Ezekiel," (2020). In her present book Herman is concerned, more specifically, with the recurring violence against and abuse of women. Her accent is on "repair," upon the rehabilitation of abused women through empowerment for an alternative life. Amid her advocacy, Herman offers two stunning summaries concerning, in turn, violence and non-violence toward vulnerable domestic partners and spouses.

Concerning *violence* and the exercise of destructive "power and control," she lists the following elements:

1. intimidation
2. emotional abuse

3. isolation
4. minimizing, denying, blaming
5. using children, with the threat of taking them away
6. using male privilege
7. using economic abuse
8. using coercion and threat (29)

The intended outcome of such strategies is the disempowerment and therefore the complete powerlessness of women. Women who are so subjected could fully understand Jeremiah's phrase, "violence and destruction."

But Herman's account is not so much focused on diagnoses as it is on restoration. Her book opens with two theses that occupy the book:

> *If trauma disorders are afflictions of the powerless, then empowerment must be a central principle of recovery. If trauma shames and isolates, then recovery must take place in community. These are the central therapeutic insights of my work, and I believe they have held up well across cultures and over time.* (2)

Thus *empowerment* through *community*!

The second inventory is her "equality wheel" that concerns movement *away from violence* toward well-being. This wheel includes:

1. non-threatening behavior
2. respect
3. trust and support
4. honesty and accountability
5. responsible parenting
6. shared responsibility
7. economic partnership
8. negotiation and fairness

The intent is to define domestic partnerships away from *control and violence* toward *equality and partnership*.

A key factor in the disempowerment of vulnerable women (or any vulnerable population including Jeremiah's triad of "alien, orphan, widow" and the poor) is to deny them speech in the public domain. As long as such speech is denied, such persons disappear from political reality and can be safely disregarded as non-persons. The pressure of silencing is constituted exactly by the elements in Herman's "wheel of power and control." (In terms of the public process of silencing, we may notice that voter repression is exactly such an act of silencing.)

Because recovery is *empowerment in community*, the most elemental act of empowerment is to restore the vulnerable and victims to speech so that they are heard and restored in the public domain. In ancient Israel it was left to the prophets—most especially Jeremiah—to sound the voice of the powerless and to summon establishment figures to notice their existence and their claim on community attention and resources. We may take Jeremiah's laments and speeches of judgment as ways of bringing victims to speech. More poignant, however, is the practice of lament that permits the victims to voice their own pain. It is for good reason that the grieving figure who speaks much in Lamentations is a woman who voices and embodies the pain and loss of "daughter Zion." Thus Jeremiah is willing and able to sound the grief in his world in order to portray what it was like to be maltreated in a world of male ruthlessness. The prophets, of course, were variously resisted and silenced, because the power structure of priests, kings, and scribes did not want the victims to be heard or noticed. Beyond that, they did not want the resources of the community to be shared with such "undeserving" voices from below. So it is in our society, that the victims of social violence in its various forms are readily women, people of color, the poor, and LGBTQ+ persons. Whenever possible, the force of *male power* is at work to intensify the vulnerability and the risk of such jeopardized populations.

And of course, in our society sits the church with its mandate to be willfully and intentionally counter-advocates. My impression is that the worship of the church is much too often a practice of what Luther has called a "Theology of Glory" in which the happy, wondrous rule of God is reiterated; the liturgy is uninterrupted and never is heard a discouraging word. I do not suggest that the well-being of this cocoon of reassurance should be broken by mouthing the judgment of God, for that only plays into the hands of authoritarianism. Rather, I suggest that the church's work in such a society as ours with its index of silence and violence is to enact always again, "a theology of the cross," that is, the articulation of those below who are the beloved of God. Thus we may, for example, permit our "theology of glory" to be interrupted by long-running wounds that have been prayed away by our habitual liturgies. And when laments are sounded in the church, we need only ask, "Who is speaking this now?" In response we may be sure that the speaker is characteristically a woman, a poor person, a person of color, or an LGBTQ+ person—someone on the bitter side of social power. Thus the church may initiate and practice such pained speech from below. Or the church may have a more specific capacity to identify, in our own community, those who might be speaking such pain. Preferable to reporting on such pain, it would be best to have, amid the liturgy, the actual carriers of such pain in our community. Such sounding of life experiences of hurt and wound, frequently or regularly, would serve to keep the church's work linked to the world that God so loved. Such a practice of "the voice of the victim" would mean, in many congregations, a break with our 'Theology of Glory" that only offers a respite from the world. But real world worship requires and permits something from us. And whenever we hear such a voice from below, we are in the vicinity of a "theology of the cross" wherein we attest that God has cast God's lot with the vulnerable. I reckon the flood narrative to be a lapse and a failure on God's part. But I imagine that by the end of the flood story God has embraced a better resolve:

> *I establish my covenant with you, that never again shall all flesh be cut off by the waters of a flood, and never again shall there be a flood to destroy the earth. God said, "This*

> *is the sign of the covenant that I make between me and you and every living creature that is with you, for all future generations. . . . I will remember my covenant that is between me and you and every living creature of all flesh; and the waters shall never again become a flood to destroy all flesh. When the bow is in the clouds, I will see it and remember the everlasting covenant between God and every living creature of all flesh that is on the earth." God said to Noah, "This is the sign of the covenant that I have established between me and all flesh that is on the earth."* (Gen 9:11–17)

This is the resolve of the creator God to avoid the wholesale savaging of the earthly population. Better that all should be saved, including the population of victims. The accent in the "theology of the cross" is the confession that God's suffering love stands in full relationship with victims. This is the story that the church performs when it breaks with a "Theology of Glory":

> *We've a story to tell to the nations,*
> *that shall turn their hearts to the right,*
> *a story of truth and mercy,*
> *a story of peace and light,*
> *a story of peace and light.* (The United Methodist Hymnal, 569)

This is a story of love wrought through "the path of sorrow" trod. It anticipates the end of evil, war, and violence. That story can be told by the church most effectively when it is narrated by those who have known powerlessness who have come anew to personal power by the recovery of their voices. What a way to think about the church: the place where silence is broken, where the truth is spoken, and where victims are empowered. That gospel tale belongs in the ears of all of God's people, and most especially on the lips of the victims now come to speech.

This economy of speech calls to mind for me Psalm 107. In the psalm, four classic cases of suffering are identified:

> *Some wandered in desert places.* (v. 4)
>
> *Some sat in darkness and in gloom,*
> *prisoners in misery and irons.* (v. 10)
>
> *Some were sick through their sinful ways.* (v. 17)
>
> *Some went down to the sea in ships.* (p. 23)

In each case, big trouble came and rendered them helpless. But in each case, they *cried out* and God saved them. We may imagine that the work of rescue was accomplished through human agents who performed God in their praxis. And in each case, those newly rescued were enjoined "to thank the Lord for his steadfast love" (Ps 107:8, 15, 21, 31). Thanks is the celebrative response of those newly empowered for an abundant life so long denied them. The church is surely the venue for such utterances as the psalm urges. The song has compelling credibility when it is on the lips of those who have newly come to life. This particular form of speech in gratitude is itself an act of empowerment, both for the speaker and for those who hear.

8

PRO-VIDEO

(For August Brueggemann)

IN OLD AGE my sleep is much too often interrupted. I cannot easily go to sleep or stay asleep. On one such restless night recently I spent my unwelcome wakefulness reminiscing about my younger years, and especially about my father August, who was a rural pastor. Thus in a flash I got these several memories of his fatherly care for me:

- My first job for pay (after mowing many lawns in our little town) was to work for Herman Brunkhorst, a grocer in town and a member of our church. (My brother Ed worked next door at the grocery store of Mr. Louis Gottenstrotter.) I was hired to be a gofer, and a stock boy who regularly swept out the store. I imagine that Mr. Brunkhorst did not really need me, but my dad quietly arranged the deal with him. I earned 83 cents a day. One day at work Mr. Brunkhorst took me to his little farm outside of town where I moved some heavy concrete blocks. I reported this routinely at home; my dad (I learned later) quietly went to Mr. Brunkhorst and told him he did not want me to do that work, as it was too heavy and that I should remain in the store. Nothing was ever said to me, and I remained at work in the store.
- I had a severe case of pneumonia in a time before penicillin. In my recovery we were scheduled to go to see Dr. Koelling in Waverly, Missouri for a check-up. My appointment happened to be the same night as a champion prize fight. I think the

match was between Joe Louis and Billy Conn, a fight that lasted not more than about twenty-four seconds. For reasons I do not now understand, I protested vigorously about missing the fight on the radio in order to see the doctor. The response of my dad was to go to the drug store and buy me a small transistor radio he could ill-afford; he was determined to have my visit to the doctor go well.

- My regular job through high school was work at a local Skelly gasoline station owned by Harry Knipmeyer. (We called it a "filling station.") I worked after school, afternoons, evenings, and on weekends. One day at work, my dad came to the station which he seldom did. He came to bring me a piece of cake. I was mightily embarrassed to have cake at work. But he said, "Your mom baked this, and we did not want you to be left out."
- Our high school basketball team consisted of ten boys. We had eleven boys in high school, but Lester Cook had a heart condition; he did not play; he was our team manager. We were not a very good team, and did not win often. (Disclosure: my brother Ed was a star on the team.) When we won a game, the young male adults in town who had previously played for the team made sure that the team was showered with free Cokes, a great treat for us. Of course they did not come around when we lost. But my dad did come around after we lost. On his parsimonious salary, he bought Cokes for the team. I suspect he wanted to say that winning or losing was not a very big deal.
- Our high school had very limited offerings. I discovered later that my dad had gone to the school board (constituted by six farmers) to insist that the school should offer Latin instruction for Ed and me. And they did so, for these two years, the only two years in the history of the school. In our first year of Latin with Mrs. Yowell, there were five of us. In the second year there were only the two of us. My dad did not know Latin, but he surmised that it was important prep work for our college years.

And that turned out to be the case, for we learned a great deal about grammar and word usage.

Thus I lay awake and was flooded with these several memories in which my dad loomed large. It struck me that what he did in all these instances was to *provide* for my well-being in attentive, generous ways. He quietly intervened on my behalf in ways that I did not know at the time. All of this came to me in the middle of the night, and I was swept up in a cascade of gratitude.

Thus in the middle of the night I thought about the word "provide," that led me to "provision," that soon led me to the word "providence." In ways that I did not know at the time, my dad's generous attentiveness to me was indeed "providential," as it set me on a course of study, work, and well-being that continues to mark my life.

Before I got back to sleep, I thought more broadly about "providence." I recalled that in a riff on Genesis 22 in *Church Dogmatics* (in a reference that is now lost to me), Karl Barth has pondered the dramatic interaction of Abraham and Isaac, a father and a son. As Abraham prepared a burnt offering, his innocent son asked him,

> *Where is the lamb for a burnt offering?* (Gen 22:7)

Abraham in faith and perhaps in perplexity, answered his sin,

> *God himself will* provide *the lamb for the burnt offering, my son.* (v. 8)

Barth imaginatively considers the fact that our word "provide" is a translation of the Hebrew word *ra'ah*, a term almost always rendered as "see." That is, God will *see it*, or God will *see to it*. And so it is reported that in the nick of time a ram appeared in the thicket to be sacrificed. As a consequence, the narrator can report:

> *So Abraham called that place "The Lord will provide"; as it is said to this day, "On the mount of the Lord it shall be provided."* (Gen 22:14)

Both times our word "provide" is a translation of *ra'ah* (see). Barth takes the usage to mean that God could see *ahead of time* what was required. He translates, "see ahead of time" as *pro-video,* thus *pro-vidence.* God knew ahead of time what is required and sees that it is given. It struck me, amid this flood of good memories, that my dad was doing exactly that provision for me, ahead of time, about which I knew very little at the time.

Next day, after some sleep and reawakening, I had a chance to think more about my dad and about God's providential care. Such thought led me back to The Evangelical Catechism in which my dad had instructed me for confirmation. The catechism attests to the simple pietism of my theological tradition. In the catechism there is not much abstract theology. Even in the first part entitled "God and his attributes," we do not get anything that we might expect about omnipotence, omnipresence, and omniscience; rather, the "attributes are "life, light, and love." What we get is a rendition of the goodness of God that is appropriate for a young teenager. With a focus on "providence," I was led to three questions in the catechism:

> *#15 How does God constantly prove himself to be the Creator?*
> ***God constantly proves himself to be the Creator by his fatherly providence, whereby he preserves and governs all things.***
>
> *#17 What does God still do for you?*
> ***God daily and abundantly provides me with all the necessaries of life, protects and preserves me from all danger.***

#18 Why does God do this for you?
God does all this out of sheer fatherly and divine goodness and mercy, without any merit or worthiness on my part.

The accent on the work of the Creator as providential led in the catechism to two suggestive scriptural citations:

The eyes of all look to you,
and you give them their food in due season.
You open your hand,
satisfying the desire of every living thing. (Ps 145:15–16)

Therefore I tell you, do not worry about your life, what you will eat or what you will drink, or about your body, what you will wear. Is not life more than food, and the body more than clothing? (Matt 6:25)

The sum of this teaching is the offer of a well-governed, generous world guaranteed by the trustworthy goodness of God. Answer #18 sounds the Reformation note of "grace alone" that is here applied to all of created reality. I have no doubt that my dad not only fully embraced this teaching, but it was the form his life took as pertained to my identity and well-being.

It occurs to me that this deep conviction of God's providential care (as instanced for me by my dad) is best sung, because it does not conform to our conventional adherence to patterns of "cause and effect." That is, it dwells outside of our common rationality and invites us to think in alternative categories. The claim of such trustworthy governance simply overrides all calculation. Thus we sing audaciously:

Be not dismayed what-e'er betide, God will take care of you;
beneath his wings of love abide, God will take care of you.

God will take care of you, through every day, o'er all the way;
he will take care of you, God will take care of you.
(The United Methodist Hymnal, 130)

We sing these words gratefully and innocently, even though we have much data to the contrary. Or we sing it defiantly, not accepting what we observe as the final reality of our lives. Or we sing with agricultural imagery:

We plow the fields and scatter
The good seed on the land,
But it is fed and watered
By God' almighty hand;
God sends the snow in winter,
The warmth to swell the grain,
The breezes and the sunshine,
And soft refreshing rain.
You only are the Maker
Of all things near and far;
You paint the wayside flower,
You light the evening star;
The winds and waves obey You,
By You the birds are fed;
Much more to us, Your children,
You give our daily bread.
We thank You, then, Creator,
For all things bright and good,
The seed-time and the harvest,
Our life, our health, our food;
Accept the gifts we offer,
For all Your love imparts,
And what You most would welcome,
Our humble, thankful hearts.
(The Presbyterian Hymnal, 560).

This hymn attunes us to the rhythms of creation upon which our lives depend.

> *As long as the earth endures,*
> *seedtime and harvest, cold and heat,*
> *summer and winter, day and night,*
> *shall not cease.* (Gen 8:22)

This hymn has dropped out of favor in more recent hymnals, likely because we mostly do not any longer live close to the cadences of the seasons; or perhaps we do not sing it because we are too aware of the ways in which the goodness of creation is so damaged and jeopardized by our technology.

Yet a third hymn that we do not sing much anymore is the stately poetry of James Russell Lowell who wrote in resistance to the slave-serving Mexican War. Here is the final stanza of what became a hymn from his poetry:

> *Though the cause of evil prosper,*
> *yet the truth alone is strong;*
> *though her portion be the scaffold,*
> *and upon the throne be wrong;*
> *yet that scaffold sways the future,*
> *and behind the dim unknown,*
> *standeth God within the shadow,*
> *keeping watch above his own.*

This final verse attests to God's hidden but certain commitment to those who have signed on for the risks and costs of God's good governance. The last lines of this verse echo for me my dad's commitment to me, "keep watching," mostly "hidden," but loving me since I was "his own."

This awakened moment in the night was a great blessing to me. It permitted me to gather together elemental truths in my life, inviting me to pass easily back and forth, as we do, between *the durable truth of the gospel* concerning the goodness of God and *the quotidian alertness of my dad.* Such back and forth is warranted by the instruction of Jesus:

> *Is there anyone among you who, if your child asks for bread, will give a stone? Or if the child asks for a fish, will give a snake? If you then, who are evil, know how to give good gifts to your children, how much more will your Father in heaven give good things to those who ask him!* (Matt 7:9–11)

I am so grateful for my dad; and then there is this "how much more" of the gospel that evokes limitless gratitude and wonder!

9

FROM "RAGTAG" TO "HOLY"

THE CROWD THAT eagerly departed Pharaoh's Egypt at the behest of YHWH was a mixed lot:

> *A mixed crowd also went up with them, and livestock in great numbers, both flocks and herds.* (Exod 12:38)

A. That crowd is termed "Israel" in the text, but the label is an anachronism, because that community still had to be formed. Before it was formed into a community with a God-given identity, the crowd had different markings:

- The crowd lacked any cohesion or identity.
- Its participants had no pedigree or qualification.
- What they had in common was the recognition that their lingering status as exploited slaves in Egypt was not right, was not bearable any longer, and had to be altered.

For good reason they had found their voice to cry out in their long-running suffering and misery:

> *The Israelites groaned under their slavery, and cried out.* (Exod 2:23)

They broke the silence imposed by Pharaoh and declared their readiness to participate in history, to be agents in the construction of their own future. The cry is generic; it sounds the pain of every human voice that has the courage to announce itself in its misery. The cry was addressed to no one in particular. That their cry arrived in the ears of YHWH, the emancipatory God, was not because of their address, but because of YHWH's capacity to attract such cries of desperate need. YHWH's ears are the sure destination of such cries across the generations.

They left as quickly as they could. They had made no preparation for departure, but simply left in a hurry. Nor had they "prepared any provisions for themselves" (Exod 12:39).

But they did not leave empty-handed:

> *They plundered the Egyptians.* (v. 36)

The verb in verse 36 is "snatch." They took what they could get their hands on from the economy of Egypt. That appropriation was "a great number of flocks and herds," real monetary value!

They trusted themselves to the wilderness beyond the reach of Pharaoh. They survived, we are told, because they received the inexplicable gift of bread from the generosity of heaven (manna) that was given by the emancipatory God. The picture we get of this harried, eager company is a snapshot of humanity in its most elemental urgency for freedom, dignity, and security. While we date the narrative, perhaps to the thirteenth century BCE, it could be in any century. It could be any moment in human history when the exploited discover that they can act with effective agency for their own future. It could be in our own time. It could be some nameless migrants seeking a safe place. It could be the #MeToo movement seeking proper constitutional rights for themselves. It could be gays and lesbians waiting impatiently for a proper place in civic discourse. It could be Native Americans seeking recovery of their own lost land. All of these populations, in every time and through history, shared an identity that is grounded in deep suffering and in bodily awareness of themselves as having a claim on the future. The Exodus narrative, with its ragtag company departing, is the most elemental human story. That story, willy-nilly, features the certifying agency of the emancipatory God without whom there is no imaginable alternative to systemic suffering. This is indeed a mixed crowd,

> without identity beyond shared departure,
> without claim beyond pain,
> without authority beyond hope, and
> without resources beyond what has been snatched from others.

This is the primal narrative of human history that we continue to recite, even those of us who live in relative comfort, dignity, and security. This is the most elemental narrative of the emancipatory God, the God who chooses as natural habitat, not the wondrous company of the other gods, but the anguished company of the left behind. This primal story is of a *mixed crowd* propelled by bold urgency, authorized by hopefulness that vetoes the governance of Pharaoh and all his predatory ilk.

B. This mixed company trusted the wilderness, sustained as they were by bread, water, and quail that were wondrously given in the desert, always at the last minute. And then, abruptly, this company is addressed by the emancipatory God via the office and mouth of Moses. This company is addressed by God's utterance and is thereby called into being and formed for the future. First, YHWH reminds this company that it was only YHWH who has made a future possible for them:

> *You have seen what I did to the Egyptians, and how I bore you on eagles' wings and brought you to myself.* (Exod 19:4)

The aim of their emancipation, it is asserted, is not the land of promise or Sinai. The destination has been "to myself!" The erstwhile slaves have been headed, from the outset, to a defining rendezvous with God.

They did not know this; it was "eagles' wings" that had transported them, from Pharaoh and on to YHWH.

But then, second, the divine address continues in future-defining authority:

> *Now therefore, if you obey my voice and keep my covenant,*
> *you shall be my treasured possession out of all the peoples.*
> *Indeed, the whole earth is mine, but you shall be for me a*
> *priestly kingdom and a holy nation.* (Exod 19:5–6)

This ragtag company without pedigree or credential invited, by the utterance of God, into a peculiar new identity:

> *treasured possession . . . kingdom of priests!*

Designated and distinguished from "all the peoples." This identity is the inverse of Hosea 1:8: This "no people" has become "my people." This staggering invite, however, is conditional: "if." The condition is specified as the emancipatory God enunciates the Ten Commandments as the norm for the new identity of this community now formed and chosen (Exod 20:1–17). These ten conditions bear no marking of class, nations, ethnicity, or cult. They are the most elemental requirements of historical well-being, grounded in a holiness that precludes every absolutism. That is all:

> *Do not impinge upon God's holiness.* (vv. 2–7)
>
> *Do two neighbor-restoring activities:*

> *Keep Sabbath.* (v. 8–11)
> *Honor parents.* (v. 12)
> *Refuse any infringement upon the neighbor: "Thou shalt not."*
> (vv. 13–17)

The commandments are a wholesale contradiction of the predatory system of Pharaoh that knew about neither *neighborliness* that refuses subservience nor about *holiness* that precludes absolutism. Pharaoh knew only about *surplus* at the cost of *subservience*. Now this new community is to eschew both *surplus* ("Do not covet") and *subservience* by treating all others as neighbors. In the tenth commandment, YHWH reiterates the term "neighbor" three times (v. 17)!

C. It did not take long, however, before this "no people" now become "my people" and took deliberate steps to guard its new identity, to protect its privileged status, and to preclude others from participation. It would have been impossible to imagine that this "mixed crowd" in the Exodus narrative would intend to exclude anyone. All could join their march toward the wilderness. But as soon as a "holy" identity is granted, it became a ground for exclusion. Thus in the "holiness" rules of Leviticus we get all kinds of exclusions of those who are judged to be unqualified. Eventually Solomon's temple, the great citadel of chosenness, would build exclusiveness into its structure as holiness is "graded" and compartmentalized into "holy of holies, holy place, and outer court" (1 Kings 6:1–6 on "vestibule, nave, and inner sanctuary"). Belatedly Israel's holy status is confirmed and to be zealously maintained:

> *Thus the* holy seed *has* mixed *itself with the peoples of the lands, and in this faithlessness the officials and leaders have led the way.* (Ezra 9:2)

It is of compelling interest that the term rendered "mixed" in this verse is the *hithpa'el* of *'arav*, not unlike *'arav* in Exodus 12:38. (The *Brown-Driver-Briggs Hebrew and English Lexicon* assigns the two words to different roots, p. 786.) However that may be, the "mixed multitude" (Exod 12:38) is now taken to be distorted by "mixing" with the peoples of the land. That is, the belated essentialism of "holy seed" now regards as a threat and distortion the very "crowd" that had at first constituted the "no people" who had become this "holy people." Thus over long centuries, the narrative of God with God's people has gone

from a *mixed crowd*,
to an odd community given a *peculiar identity and vocation*,
to a "*holy seed*" that must be protected through attentive exclusions.

The sequence is breathtaking. It is as though it was necessary for "the holy people" to forget its origin, to fail to remember that its life with YHWH began with a surge of unidentified nobodies seeking an alternative life. In such amnesia, the belated community can refuse and resist the various companies of nobodies from which it was, by the generosity of YHWH, initially constituted.

Of course the same dramatic sequence is readily re-performed. It is re-performed in the life of the church as the ragtag company gathered around Jesus became a community (see Luke 7:22, 19:48). That company that was "not a people" became "God's people" (1 Pet 2:10). That community was given a defining purpose in the world to refuse conformity to the world, and to be about the work of transformation by acts of generosity, hospitality, and returning good for evil (Rom 12:1–21). It did not take very long, however, before this missional community formed from ragtag folk drawn to Jesus became self-aware of its "Holy, Catholic" status that it took steps to protect and guard. It was not long before the church took on the onerous work of exclusivity in order to maintain its "holiness."

The same sequence can be readily traced concerning the immigrants who came to America. We know that those who came included the land-hungry fortune seekers, many of whom were rejects and losers in the Old World. But very soon that white Euro-identity was formed into a freedom-loving community, a privilege-guarding enterprise. And not long after that the white power establishment began to worry about the arrival of all the immigrants who posed a threat to "holy whiteness," so that barriers and quotas came to be enacted in order to protect the homogeneity of race and ethnicity that was easily converted into a particular kind of nationalism. That worry of distortion by "mixing" did not for the moment extend to the masses of Black Africans who were forcibly brought to our land for the sake of cheap labor.

From this oft-repeated dramatic sequence, two extrapolations occur to me. First, concerns our US denominationalism. Long ago Richard Niebuhr, *The Social Sources of Denominationalism* (1922), traced the way in which socioeconomic and historical factors produced US denominations and a general shared readiness to excommunicate all who embodied otherwise. Thus the church has been formed among us through the pressures of linguistic, ethnic, and economic realities that could then claim grounding in tradition. One might indeed pray and hope for a fresh Pentecost in which the Spirit of God may break through our varied barriers into a redress that "all may be one":

> *At this sound the crowd gathered and was bewildered, because each one heard them speaking in the native language of each. Amazed and astonished, they asked, "Are not all these who are speaking Galileans? And how is it that we hear, each of us, in our own native language? Parthians, Medes, Elamites, and residents of Mesopotamia, Judea and Cappadocia, Pontus, and Asia, Phrygia, and Pamphylia, Egypt and the parts of Libya belonging to Cyrene, visitors from Rome, both Jews and proselytes, Cretans and Arabs—in our languages we hear them speaking about God's deeds of power.* (Acts 2:6–11)

The facts on the ground, however, suggest that we have a mighty capacity to refuse such a Spirit-propelled possibility. Indeed, it is rather diminishment of institutional power and resources that requires our several tribes/sects to find each other, and to come together in common confession and mission. Such necessity, perhaps Spirit-compelled, leads us, always belatedly, to discern that what unites our several sects is more than what divides us. Sometimes we come to awareness that what binds us together is enough to join together as alternative to the demonic forces of the predatory economy all around us. Through this process we can observe that the church is yet again like ancient Israel, constituted by a ragtag company of those who have been summoned to an alternative identity and mission. In ancient Israel there were not many among that ragtag company who were "wise, or powerful, or of noble birth" (1 Cor 1:26). So also in the early church God chose "the weak and the foolish" to be God's own people. The current missional crisis (lack of people and money) in the church is perhaps the way of the Spirit to lead us again to our rootage and our proper calling, without the leverage of power and wealth. We may pause over the wonder that God has a readiness to form a "people" out of "no people."

Second, it occurs to me that the same may be said of our national identity as "Americans" or as the principle carriers of the culture of "the West." Naoíse Mac Sweeny, *The West: A New History in Fourteen Lives* (2023) writes of "the grand narrative of the West":

> *It was deeply embedded in the political rhetoric of the new United States, providing an ideological basis on which the revolutionaries could argue for liberty and an end to imperialism on the one hand, whilst simultaneously preserving internal structures of oppression and colonialism on the other.* (245)

We are, we may anticipate, in the last throes of the struggle against white supremacy, but the work is clearly not yet completed. Mac Sweeny presents fourteen sketches of particular persons that run all the way from Herodotus (the ancient historian) to Francis Bacon (the seventeenth-century English "scientist"), to Edward Said (a contemporary Palestinian-American academic). This author shows that for all the exclusively "Western" claims of being heir to Greek and Roman culture, in fact "The West," and so America, has been a strong mix of many peoples who are not only from Europe, but also from Asia and Africa. Thus the imagined claims of purity and supremacy are destructive fictions. In truth American nationalism is constituted by many peoples from many places of origin with all kinds of ethnic and national rootage. We are indeed, historically and practically, *a mixed company* clustered as a unity by a summons to "a more perfect union" that overrides and transcends all of our cherished particularities.

I submit that this drama of "*no people—my people—holy people*" is a drama worth our attention, as we continue to re-perform it in present time. We may well remember that we have been formed as a nation out beyond our cherished origins. We may indeed remember—and be grateful, and have fresh courage for the work yet to be done. The great missional mandate to the church stems from this wondrous reality that God desires to choose "the weak and the foolish" to do the transformative work in the world that is never done by the wise and the powerful.

10

CASCADE! DIVINE?

TWO SEASONED, DISCERNING critics of our environmental crisis have written something of a manifesto concerning the urgent need for better, more responsible policies that care for the earth. Their statement is entitled, *An Inconvenient Apocalypse: Environmental Collapse, Climate Crisis, and the Fate of Humanity* (2022). Wes Jackson and Robert Jensen see that the coming climate disaster is apocalyptic in scope. And they play with Al Gore's understated term "inconvenient," as they see that coming disaster as much deeper than "inconvenient." They fully understand how the environmental crisis is systemically related to a host of other human crises as well. Thus they offer the eye-catching phrase, "multiple cascading crises" (4).

Their index of coming crises is much more than "inconvenient"; it is reality-altering in the most comprehensive ways:

- The decline of key natural resources and an emerging global resource crisis, especially in water
- The collapse of ecosystems that support life, and the mass extinction of species
- Human population growth and demand, beyond the earth's carrying capacity
- Global warming, sea-level rise, and changes in the earth's climate affecting all human capacity
- Universal pollution of the earth system and all life by chemicals
- Rising food insecurity and failing nutritional quality
- Nuclear arms and other weapons of mass destruction
- Pandemics of new and untreatable diseases
- The advent of powerful, uncontrolled new technologies

- National and global failure to understand and act preventively on these risks. (10)

They see that such crises will evoke the formulation of a new economic order:

> *If we don't transcend a growth economy, there are hard times ahead. And if we do manage to construct a new economic order, there are hard times ahead. Hard times are coming for everyone, even though some people are more responsible for social and ecological problems than others and some of those people will be able to evade the consequences of those problems, at least in the short run.*
>
> *The task of creating new systems is daunting, in large part because of challenges posed by the nature of the human animal, combined with most people's denial of what it means to be an animal. We have faith in the better angels of our nature but realize that those better angels alone won't save us from what we call "the temptations of dense energy," which have come most recently in the form of fossil fuels. We conclude that there are no workable solutions to the most pressing problems of our historical moment.* (10)

I have in particular latched on to their remarkable phrase, "multiple cascading crises." What follows here is a reflection on a particular biblical text that was called to my mind by that phrase. I exposit this text in a playful way so that I do not intend to draw a conclusion or teach a lesson, but only to live with this innocent-looking text to experience the cumulative force of such a cascade that reaches for Job in the proportion of a tsunami.

The text of Job 1:13–19 is part of a "folk tale" in the book of Job that frames the poetry that follows. The "folk tale" gives us a glimpse of the governing power of the creator God, which is concealed from Job. God is unnamed in these verses though verse 16 allows a conventional phrase, "the fire of God." It is often noted that in the prologue and the epilogue of Job, God is called by the Israelite name, YHWH. That naming of YHWH anchors the book of Job in the Israelite tradition, even though in the poetry of Job God is not so identified. In any case, behind the narrative is the governing force and will of the creator God who makes covenant with Israel.

These narrative verses are terse, disciplined, and focused on the dramatic repetition in a four-fold manner. The four decisive moments occur quickly in sequence. After the first crisis (vv. 13–15), the second is while the messenger "was still speaking" (v. 16). And so the third (v. 17), and so the fourth one (v. 18). They are in sequence but almost simultaneous in their reporting, so that the listener has no chance to catch a breath between the arrival of the several messengers of bad news. The prose narrative clearly intends that we should experience the "cascade" of calamities that come directly and abruptly upon the family and property of Job. In the background is the bet of Satan with God that these destructive "touches" will cause Job to curse God (1:11). Later on in chapter 2, after that bet of Satan has failed, Satan ups the ante, betting that a "touch" on Job's body will lead him to curse God. As the matter unfolds, Job comes very close to cursing God in 3:1–26, but not quite!

Our interest, however, is fixed on the four afflictions on Job's family and property in this first test of Satan's bet. The disciplined repetition of the sequence of crises wears away at Job's faith and the fabric of his social world. The narrative proceeds step-by-step to let the cadences of repetition have their full sway.

Each of the four episodes, quick as they are, has a clear beginning and ending.

The beginning:

A messenger (Job 2:13)
another (v. 16)
another (v. 17)
another (v. 18)

The ending:

> I alone have escaped to tell you (v. 15)
> I alone have escaped to tell you (v. 16)
> I alone have escaped to tell you (v. 17)
> I alone have escaped to tell you (v. 18)

The assault:

> the Sabeans (v. 15)
> the fire of God v. 16)
> the Chaldeans (v. 17)
> a great wind (v. 18)

In the four cases we have an alteration of an

> historical enemy,
> "natural cause,"
> historical enemy, and
> "natural cause."

The two alternatives of "history" and "nature" are equivalent. Both exist and operate according to the governance of the creator God. In context it was Satan, in concert with God, who initiated this cascade of crises.

The result:

> oxen and donkeys carried off; servants killed (Job 2:15)
> sheep burned up, servants consumed (v. 16)
> camels carried off, servants killed (v. 17)
> sons and daughters—young people—dead (v. 19; see v. 13)

The sequence is framed by "sons and daughters" in verses 13 and 19. In both cases they are children of privilege, "eating and drinking" (vv. 13, 19).

The cadence of the report with "killed, killed, killed, dead" and "carried off, burned, carried off, struck" sounds fully and decisively, not unlike the dull thud of a bell tolling. We get no comment or elaboration. Indeed, all we get is the report that Job, in a tone of resignation, defies Satan's bet:

> *Naked I came from my mother's womb, and naked shall I return there; the Lord gave, and the Lord has taken away; blessed be the name of the Lord.* (Job 1:21)

In the poetry that follows we can trace Job's response to this cascade of crises that in chapter 2 is reinforced with Satan's heavy "touch" of,

> *loathsome sores on Job from the sole of his foot to the crown of his head.* (Job 2:7)

Even now, Job will not curse God. Job offers three responses to this cascade of trouble.

First, he complains bitterly and at length. He does not doubt that the troubles come from God. He is, moreover, deeply inured in the retrograde notion of "deeds and consequences." He vigorously denies he has done anything to evoke such consequences.

Second, he offers a compelling defense of his own innocence (31:1–40). And nowhere in the book of Job is his innocence brought into question.

Third, Job is finally addressed by God in the whirlwind. He has been eagerly asking for and demanding an encounter with the Holy One as an opportunity to defend himself (see 31:35–37). The confrontation offered by God, however, takes Job completely by surprise. The creator God has no interest at all in Job's case. God will not defend the justice or injustice of God's treatment of Job. Instead, God will, in boastful bombast, assert God's own powerful preemption that reduces Job to trifling presence before God. The great doxologies of Job 38–41 in God's own mouth are not designed to persuade Job as much as to overwhelm him. And overwhelm him they did! In his first, feeble response Job will not defend himself and makes no answer at all (40:3–5). He is quick to see that a defense of himself is an irrelevance in this context of God's overwhelming self-assertion. In his second response we are given an enigmatic reply that defies our decoding (42:1-6). We are able to see, nonetheless, that in his response Job *repositions himself* before the creator God and accepts his status as *a penultimate creature* for whom his cocksure confidence in the "deeds-consequences" ethical system is seen to be an irrelevance. Job's ethical self-confidence is blown away by the awesomeness and wonder of creation as God's creaturely work. Thus after *complaint*, Job accepts *repositioning*. In that new posture he is commended as "speaking what is right" (42:7–8). He is restored to wealth and prosperity (42:12–14). We may wonder, in his belated restoration, how he thought about the four-fold assault on his life. Surely in his aging well-being, he could still vividly recall his pain and loss that could never be covered over by restoration.

My thought is that we should not permit the rest of Job to let us retreat too quickly from the cascade of crises (1:13–19). We may linger there a while in the recognition that crises do come upon us in inexplicable ways that violate every code of explanation we could muster. At the end of Job's fourth episode, the narrator is silent. And Job is silent. And we are left speechless before the cascade of troubles that strikes us, always yet again as incommensurate to our actual living. Or so we readily conclude.

For the moment let us entertain the interface between this four-fold cascade of crises and the index of crises enumerated by Jackson and Jenson. Like that ancient four-fold assault, our cascade of crises comes without explanation or justification. And like that four-fold assault, ours end in dread-filled loss that is beyond our reckoning.

Perhaps we could imagine ourselves making a response not unlike that of Job:

- Like Job, *we can complain.* We can complain against the fiscal and technological powers that cause our cascade; but then we notice our own complicity with them in benefitting from the cascade. We are not likely to blame God for these troubles as we are too wise and knowing for such innocence. No weather-reporter will credit God with bad weather, scientifically informed as they are. But occasionally a weather-reporter will slip to say, "This is a storm of biblical proportion." This is surely a soft euphemism for "God caused," but no scientifically educated weather reporter will say that. But still! We are haunted by a hidden, powerful mystery that is beyond our ken whom we may suspect has agency. It is an awkward, timid suspicion, because it violates our best Enlightenment learning. That trace of suspicion, however, will not easily and finally go away, and so we are pressed to euphemism. Thus first, we complain about the cause of the cascade and we think we mostly know whom to blame.
- Second, like Job, we may *do a morality check* to determine our innocence in the matter. And if we lack a systemic view of things, we may conclude that we are innocent and not implicated concerning the cascade of crises. However, we are not so easily acquitted, because our common collusion in such matters is easy enough to see. Thus we do not receive the word from the whirlwind with an easy conscience.
- But third, like Job, we are *addressed by holy mystery* amid the cascade. We are brought up short with our lack of understanding and our own sense of awe:

O Lord my God, when I in awesome wonder,
Consider all the worlds Thy Hands have made;
I see the stars, I hear the rolling thunder,

Thy power throughout the universe displayed.
Then sings my soul, My Saviour God to Thee,
How great Thou art, how great Thou art.
Then sings my soul, My Saviour God to Thee,
How great Thou art, How great Thou art!
("How Great Thou Art," The United Methodist Hymnal, 77*)*

If we receive that stunning wonder of the cascade, we may indeed arrive at awe appropriate to our status. As a consequence, we may then come to a fresh awareness of our penultimate status in the universe and for an instant turn away from our Promethean self-deception of mastery. Such a "turning away" from our illusion of mastery could amount to refusing to trust ourselves to technological mastery and control, and return us to our proper role alongside the other creatures. While we need not think the cascade of crises is designed pedagogically, we can nonetheless learn from it and accept a more modest role in the management of God's creation. So it was for Job as he was left in a new state of well-being, "full of days" (42:17) when,

the Lord blessed the latter day of Job more than his beginning. (Job 42:12)

None of that, to be sure, is on the horizon in our dramatic, symmetrical text of 1:13–19. In that text we have only the bare outline of the cascade of crises. That text is the beginning point for Job to "come to himself" and accept his proper place in God's creation. We also might use our cascade of crises for such learning. I do not need to tell you that such learning will require the good pedagogy that can only come in the context of faith.

As I reflected on Job in his Promethean self-assurance and in his fresh repositioning in penultimacy, I was led to the beginning of Paul's ode to *agape-love*. As you know, Paul writes:

> *If I speak in the tongues of mortals and of angels, but do not have love, I am a noisy gong or a clanging cymbal. And if I have prophetic powers, and understand all mysteries and all knowledge, and if I have all faith, so as to remove mountains, but do not have love, I am nothing.* (1 Cor 13:1–2)

In our technological capacity we have knowledge to "remove mountains." When such mastery lacks love, it goes awry. Paul's bid is that everything is different when there is self-giving love. We have no explicit evidence that Job turned to *agape-love*, but we may imagine that he mutated in his passion for mastery, control, and possession. No wonder he was more blessed in his latter days!

Part III

THE ONE POWER

11

FULL OF DAYS!

THIS IS THE reflection of an old man who has likely completed his work, perhaps my final effort at a blog. I have been pondering of late the biblical formula for a life fully lived and brought to a fitting end in a timely death. The preferred biblical formulation is "full of days." The formula is frequently utilized for life closure in the Bible. It occurs to me that the formula suggests more than a long life. It affirms as well that the life now ending is one of some import and substance. Thus:

- Isaac died after 180 years:

> *And Isaac breathed his last; he died and was gathered to his people, old and* full of days*; and his sons Esau and Jacob buried him.* (Gen 35:29)

His life was fulfilled, in patriarchal fashion, by the birth of his two sons. He was able, moreover, to witness the reconciliation of the twins after a family-dividing rift (33:1–11). The reconciliation persisted, even if the two brothers went their separate ways. Abraham, Isaac's father, receives a life-ending formula that is differently articulated, the only instance of it of which I know:

> *Abraham breathed his last and died in a good old age, an old man and* full of years, *and was gathered to his people.* (Gen 25:8)

- David died at the end of a long, successful reign of forty years:

> *He died in a good old age,* full of days, *riches, and honor; and his son Solomon succeeded him.* (1 Chron 29:28)

(The comparable report in 1 Kings 1:10–12 cites no such formula.) David's days were indeed "full." As stated here, full of riches and honors; but also filled with piety, violence, and endless contestation. Even his death, as narrated in 1 Kings 1–2, was a matter of violent cunning and manipulation. In this report, his ending was successful beyond all sorts of vagaries that had marked his vexed life.

- The concluding formula concerning the life of Job's narrative ends in the same way:

And Job died, old and full of days. (Job 42:17)

At the end, Job's life was filled with well-being: seven sons, three beautiful daughters, fourteen thousand sheep, six thousand camels, a thousand yoke of oxen, a thousand donkeys; all of this in abundance. He continues to be the "quantifier" who ends with the most! But of course Job's life had been full of vexation, trouble, and suffering. In that earlier vexation, Job could lament:

A mortal, born of woman,
few of days and full of trouble,
comes up like a flower and withers,
flees like a shadow and does not last.
(Job 14:1; see Ecclesiastes 2:3)

He remains, however, a man of loss, including the loss of property and of children (1:13–19). That loss does not detract from the affirmative formula of closure at the end. It is as though, in this rendering, Job's well-being had outlasted his loss and suffering. We are not told how he continued to carry his grief for the children whom he never recovered.

The most interesting usage of our formula concerns the priest Jehoiada. He is reported to have been the sponsor and protector of the boy king, Joash (2 Kgs 11:4–8). He was, moreover, responsible for supervising and financing the renovation and restoration of the temple in Jerusalem (vv. 9–12). In the version of his narrative in Chronicles, his bio concludes:

> *But Jehoiada grew old and* full of days, *and died; he was one hundred thirty years old at his death. And they buried him in the city of David among the kings, because he had done good in Israel, and for God and his house.* (2 Chron 24:15–16)

He was one of a kind in the narrative of Israel, and duly honored to rank, in death, alongside the kings. He did "good" in Israel! The summary includes a triad, *good in Israel, good for God, good for his house* (temple).

His life of faithfulness, however, had no durable effect in Israel. The next paragraph reports that upon his death:

> *They abandoned the house of the Lord, the God of their ancestors, and served the sacred poles and the idols.* (v. 18)

The paragraph is a summary of the recurring Deuteronomic pattern of transgression, prophetic summons, and refusal to listen. In response to the apostasy of the royal house, Zedekiah, the son of Jehoiada, spoke out in prophetic fashion:

> *Thus says God: Why do you transgress the commandments of the Lord, so that you cannot prosper? Because you have forsaken the Lord, he has also forsaken you.* (v. 20)

His son's warning, however, only provoked hostility that led to the violent death of the son of the priest. The narrative reports:

> *King Joash did not remember the* kindness *that Jehoiada, Zechariah's father had shown him but killed his son. As he was dying, he said, "May the Lord see and avenge!"* (v. 22)

The king whom Jehoiada had sponsored and protected departed from the way of the Torah that he had advocated. The worship of "sacred poles" and idols is a religious manifestation of socioeconomic policies that disregarded covenantal neighborliness. The concluding formula of verse 22 includes the term "kindness" that renders *hesed*. That is, the king did not remember or embrace the covenantal accents of the tradition of Jehoiada, and joined in the recurring apostasy of the Davidic house. It was for good reason that the days of the priest were "full," full of faithfulness to the Torah that held the royal house to covenantal norms.

All of these characters—Isaac, David, Job, and Jehoiada—died well, as they had lived well. Hans Walter Wolff, *Anthropology of the Old Testament* (1974) shrewdly observes that the formula "full of days" does not mean "satiated." Rather, it means "satisfied." Lives lived in fidelity are lives that end "satisfied." The inverse is readily inferred. Lives lived out of the reach of such faithfulness end in dissatisfaction. As is well known, in the Old Testament no "reward" is on offer or expected beyond such satisfaction. It is enough to have lived well and "fully."

I am glad, near the end of my life, to draw near to this formula of well-being. My days have indeed been full, and are full. Such a claim for myself does not, for an instant, overlook or disregard my many failings of both omission and commission. So it was for those who took comfort in the formula in the old narrative. So I end with some satisfaction; but much more, I end in gratitude, both to God and to the rich, abundant company of human agents who have filled my life with goodness and well-being. My life has been "full of days," so much more than I could ask or expect.

- My life has been filled with good generative teachers: Lillian Cott, Esther Yowell, Th. W. Mueller, Lionel Whiston Jr., and James Muilenburg among them.
- My life has been filled with good work, all the way from my first job at mowing lawns (thirteen of them including the city park),

to teaching at my two beloved seminaries with good colleagues and good students.

- My life has been filled (not like that of David) with an overflow of riches and honor, but with more than enough recognition to affirm my working life, not least to have been elected as President of the Society of Biblical Literature.
- My life has overflowed with many good friends.
- My life has been confirmed with good students, among them those who have followed me into Old Testament study—Bobby, David, Davis, John, Jonathan, Mark, Nancy, Scott, Tim, and Tod.
- My life has been greatly blessed to see my five grandchildren generatively and productively launched toward adulthood: Christiana, August, Emilia, Anabelle, and Peter.
- My life is full in the assurance that my two well-beloved sons, Jim and John, are fully functioning, knowing, generative, and caring adults.
- My life has been crowned by the deep love that my wife Tia manifests daily toward me by which I am sustained with a semblance of well-being. I am indeed "full of days." I may (and expect to) live yet a while, but one never knows. It is a fullness that is complete for me. It is full enough to evoke from me an echo of Simeon's *Nunc Dimittis*:

> *Master, now you are dismissing your servant in peace,*
> *according to your word;*
> *for my eyes have seen your salvation,*
> *which you have prepared in the presence of all peoples,*
> *a light for revelation to the Gentiles*
> *and for the glory to your people Israel.* (Luke 2:29–32)

Of course my "seeing," unlike that of Simeon, is from afar. I can more easily and readily join in the "anthem" of my German evangelical antecedents:

Now thank we all our God with heart and hands and voices,
who wondrous things hath done, in whom this world rejoices;
who, from our mothers' arms, hath blessed us on our way
with countless gifts of love and still is ours today.
O may this bounteous God through all our lives be near us,
with ever joyful hearts and blessed peace to cheer us;
and keep us in God's grace, and guide us when perplexed,
and free us from all ills in this world and the next.
All praise and thanks to God who reigns in highest heaven,
to Father and to Son and Spirit now be given;
the one eternal God, whom heaven and earth adore,
the God who was, and is, and shall be evermore. (Glory to God, 643)

"From my mother's arms" I have been blessed on the way. I have received "countless gifts of love," still today! Like my forebears, I can end with "all thanks and praise to God."

12

GROWING IN GRACE

MATTHEW 5:17–19 IS A signature expression of the primary accents of Matthew's gospel:

> *Do not think that I have come to abolish the law or the prophets; I have come not to abolish but to fulfill. For truly I tell you, until heaven and earth pass away, not one letter, not one stroke of a letter, will pass from the law until all is accomplished. Therefore, whoever breaks one of the least of these commandments and teaches others to do the same, will be called least in the kingdom of heaven; but whoever does them and teaches them will be called great in the kingdom of heaven.*

This paragraph situates Jesus squarely in the Torah tradition of Judaism; it insists on scrupulous and attentive honoring of the commandments. And it articulates Jesus as the one who "fulfills—completes—perfects" Jewish Torah. This testimony refuses to distinguish between gradations of commandments and embraces all of them. Matthew is easily the "most Jewish" of the gospels and invites us to discern Jesus as a decisive performer of Jewish faith. But then verse 20 draws my particular attention:

> *For I tell you, unless your righteousness exceeds that of the scribes and Pharisees, you will never enter the kingdom of heaven.* (v. 20)

Jesus summons his followers to outdo Jewish experts on the Torah in their seriousness about Torah obedience. This "greater righteousness" suggests *levels of seriousness* about the obedient conduct of one's life.

When I reflected on this suggestion of gradations or levels of moral seriousness, the first thing I thought of was "stages of growth" in the defining work of the great Swiss child psychologist, Jean Piaget. In a series of books in the mid-twentieth century, Piaget reported on his careful observation of children and concluded that children in their intellectual and moral development regularly advance through several different stages of learning:

Sensorimotor stage: Birth to two years
Preoperational stage: Ages two to seven
Concrete operational stage: Ages seven to eleven
Formal operational stage: Ages twelve and up

These are quite "normal" and "natural" stages of development. Once identified, they can be variously observed in a child by any parent or educator. Piaget regarded his articulation as descriptive of a process through which a child moves quite freely and unwittingly.

Piaget's work, along with the articulation of Erik Erikson and Lawrence Kohlberg's stages of moral development were taken up by James W. Fowler. In his book, *Stages of Faith: Psychology of Human Development and the Quest for Meaning* (1981). Fowler reads the sequence of "stages of development" from a religious perspective with a great accent on the moral. He proposes that moral maturation and moral development include the following:

Birth to age two: Primal Undifferentiated Faith
Stage 1 (Ages three to seven): Intuitive-Projective Faith
Stage 2 (Ages seven to twelve): Mythic-Literal Faith
Stage 3 (Age twelve to adult): Synthetic Conventional Faith
Stage 4 (Mid-twenties to late thirties): Reflective Faith
Stage 5 (Midlife crisis): Conjunctive Faith
Stage 6 (Later adulthood): Universalizing Faith (or Enlightenment).

Fowler's work gained great popularity in the church. Amid the many interpretations of his work, his "stages" ran the risk of being taken not as "descriptive," as Piaget had insisted, but as prescriptive, as tasks of growth to be accomplished. Thus there was from Fowler a suggestion (perhaps because of a Wesleyan tilt), that human persons have a responsibility or an obligation to seek to grow, and to make an effort to grow in one's moral capacity and sensibility.

The matter of "descriptive" and "prescriptive" in Piaget, Kohlberg, and Fowler is complex and tricky. If the processes are "normal" and "natural," then there is no imperative attached to them. But conversely, if they are prescriptive, then they are not "normal" or "natural," but require resolve and effort. It is to be recognized, of course, that the matter of moral development occurs in ways that we cannot discern, so that the matter is open to endless adjudication.

But what stands out in Matthew 5:20, in light of this work on "moral development," is the fact that Jesus's word to his disciples does include an urgent imperative. That is, the disciples are called to account for their capacity for and practice of "righteousness." This accent on responsibility for the practice of one's "righteousness" is worth noting, especially in a Christian context wherein we have long since championed "grace alone" as the truth of our moral life. This theological tradition has been haunted by the specter of "works righteousness," and has largely eschewed any notion of such responsibility. Indeed, the church has so stressed "grace alone" and left off the imperatives of the gospel, so that we have ended, more or less, in "cheap grace." That phrase from Dietrich Bonhoeffer concerns not just a general indulgence; in his context it concerned a capacity for church people to accommodate Nazi ideology in the scope of the gospel. In the same way in the US church there is an easy capacity to affirm, within faith, all manner of ideology such as racism, or nationalism, or capitalism. The church becomes so welcoming that the demands of the gospel evaporate in a general offer of welcome, friendliness, and good feeling. It may be that such a stance is important, given that our Puritan-based culture is rigorous in some of its expressions. And yet Jesus—without benefit of Piaget or Fowler—and without adjudicating "description-prescription," summons his disciples to a "greater righteousness." Such a summons suggests that the church has work to do in schooling its members in the arts and practices of righteousness, with anticipation that we are, as a congregation, engaged in the work of moral growth beyond our easy inclination. The words of Jesus suggest that disciplines can be practiced, habits can be formed, and decisions can be made that lead to "greater righteousness."

One remarkable expression of this imperative is the teaching of the Westminster Larger Catechism on the subject:*

> *Q. 167: How is our baptism to be improved by us?*
>
> *Answer: The needful but much neglected duty of improving our Baptism, is to be performed by us all our life long, especially in the time of temptation, and when we are present at the administration of it to others, by serious and thoughtful consideration of the nature of it, and of the ends for which Christ instituted it, the privileges and benefits conferred and sealed thereby, and our solemn vow made therein; by being humbled by our sinful defilement, our falling short of, and walking contrary to, the grace of the Baptism and our engagements; by growing up to assurance of pardon of sin, and of all other blessings sealed to us in that Sacrament; by drawing strength from the death and resurrection of Christ, into whom we are baptized, for the mortifying of sin, and quickening of grace; and by endeavoring to live by faith, to have our conversation in holiness and righteousness, as those that have therein given up their names to Christ; and to walk in brotherly love, as being baptized by the same Spirit into one body.*

---

* I had a clue about this phrase, "improving our baptism," but relied on Erskine Clarke to help me locate it in the catechism.

This astonishing phrase, "improving our baptism" accepts that serious believers are engaged in reflective growth in order to more fully embrace and practice the alternative life to which we are summoned in the gospel. The answer in the catechism is filled with active imperative verbs:

> *be humbled by our sin;*
> *growing up to assurance of pardon;*
> *drawing strength from the death and new life of Jesus;*
> *endeavoring to live by faith; and*
> *walking in brotherly love.*

The catechism has no doubt that such prospects are on offer in and through the sacrament. These several summons are in the orbit of baptism, the entry point into and marker of an alternative life. Thus I suppose that every congregation and every pastor might thoughtfully and endlessly adjudicate the matter of "cheap grace" (that readily accommodates our ideological waywardness) and "works righteousness" (that presumes too much on our own merit. My own observation of the church is that it is the latter that most readily besets us, as though the gospel were a free offer of "love sweet love," without any summons to new life attached to it. My thought is that such pastors and congregations might consider how and in what ways participants in the life of the congregation are being equipped and given the skills and sensibility that make an alternative life possible that knowingly contradicts the common life of our culture.

I finish this reflection with reference to three scriptural recitations. First, Paul, the great advocate of "grace alone," twice in his letter to the Philippians attests the urgency of growth in faith. In Philippians 2, after the great hymn of the humbled-exalted Lord (2:5–11), Paul follows with a "therefore":

> *Therefore, my beloved, just as you have always obeyed me,*
> *not only in my presence, but much more now in my absence,*

> *work out your own salvation with fear and trembling; for it is God who is at work in you, enabling you both to will and to work for his good pleasure.* (2:12–13)

He addresses the congregation as "my beloved," and commends their obedience. Then he voices the great imperative:

> *Work out your own salvation.*

The operational verb, *katergzethe*, means to "achieve, accomplish, produce, create." That is, one's "salvation," one's happy linkage to the God of the gospel, is one's proper work. Paul anticipates his congregation will be at the task. They will, moreover, do so with "fear and trembling," that is, with awareness that this is an urgent high-risk task. But before he finishes his pastoral urging, Paul comes around to affirm that it is God "at work" (*evergon*) who enables your work. Thus it is a both/and, not without human effort, not without divine engagement.

In the next chapter Paul takes up the mandate he has voiced in chapter 2, and makes the matter quite personal for himself:

> *Not that I have already obtained this or have already reached the goal; but I press on to make it my own, because Christ Jesus has made me his own. Beloved, I do not consider that I have made it my own, but this one thing I do: forgetting what lies behind and straining forward to what lies ahead, I press toward the goal for the prize of the heavenly call of God in Christ Jesus.* (Phil 3:12–14)

He utilizes strong verbs of effort to describe his own continuing resolve to grow in faith:

> *press on*
>
> *strive*
>
> *press on*

He is unambiguously clear about "the gospel": "the heavenly call of God in Christ Jesus." Paul sees that his life is to be given over to a purpose well beyond himself or his own "natural, normal" inclination, a purpose that requires his deepest attentiveness. He anticipates that he will continue to "mature" as a member of the body of Christ, and he will give his energy to that role and identity. He urges his addressees at Philippi to new diligence, to assure we do not yield to "what we have attained" (3:16).

Finally, I cite a narrative that evidences the kind of "greater righteousness" to which Jesus is committed (Matt 19:16–30, Mark 10:17–31, Luke 18:18–30). A serious man puts a question to Jesus (Matt 19:16). Jesus answers the man with the commandments (vv. 17–19). The commandments he names are intended to be an allusion to the entire corpus of the Torah. Notably, his final one is "love of neighbor, not among the "Ten" of Sinai. The man compliments himself for being a serious, effective Torah-keeper (v. 20). The conversation might have ended there. The man embodies "the righteousness of the scribes and Pharisees" (see 5:20). But the man knows he has not yet received all that Jesus has to tell him. He asks for more (19:20). He lacks what would make him "perfect" (*teleios*) (v. 21); this is the same term as used in Matthew 5:17. And then Jesus responds to the man and delivers his zinger:

> *If you wish to be perfect (*teleios*), go, sell your possessions, and give the money to the poor, and you will have treasure in heaven; then come, follow me.* (Matt 19:21)

Five quick imperatives: "go, sell, give, come, follow." This is the "righteousness" that exceeds conventional Judaism. The summons of Jesus is to divest of this world's riches, to trade them for an alternative treasure that has currency only in the alternative world where the governance of God prevails. This imperative gives unmistakable substance to the notion of the "greater righteousness" of 5:20. This righteousness is not about being "good" or being "pure" or being "holy" in any conventional sense. It is only about the poor, about provision for the poor and making resources available for the well-being of the poor.

The response of the man to the mandate of Jesus is no big surprise, for it is the response we all easily make. The hindrance to the alternative life of Jesus is "many possessions," perhaps monetary, but of many other kinds as well. It is our "many possessions" that can be kept intact by diligent rule-keeping that are at issue in the "greater righteousness." The disciples who observed this interaction got the point. It is hard! It is too hard! It requires a big effort, but it is too hard. But Jesus is ready for the shock of the disciples as they discern, yet again, what it is for which they have signed on. At least the disciples, unlike the man, did not turn away because it is too hard. They stayed for the follow up session and in this their moment of astonishment. Jesus repositions the shock of the disciples amid the overriding power of God's goodness:

> *For mortals it is impossible, but for God all things are possible.* (Matt 19:26)

This is the same both/and we have seen elsewhere. Such "righteousness" is demanding of human effort. But such "righteousness" is the work of the God of all possibility. The response of Jesus is quite like the summons of Paul:

> *Work out your own salvation, for God is at work in you!*

The trajectory of both/and—both human effort and divine goodness—is the truth of our faith. It is such an urgent truth in a culture that wants to settle for the cheap grace of self-indulgence or for the fearful effort of works righteousness. The way to greater righteousness is neither of these. Rather, it is the slow work of permitting the good power of God's transformative grace to be at work amid our attentive disciplines in faith. This is the good work a congregation can do as it summons and empowers its members to grow in grace. What a phrase: "improve your baptism"! The imperative is to let our faith identity become more complete. As we grow in such grace, we may contribute to the formation of a sociopolitical economy in which the poor receive good news, even as the blind, lame, deaf, and lepers have transformative restoration (Matt 11:5). It is our work through which the restorative work of God is done.

13

LIKE OIL RUNNING DOWN, LIKE DEW ON THE MOUNTAIN

(For Edward Brueggemann)

MY BROTHER ED completed the foursome of our family. When I remember Ed, it is easy for me to suggest Psalm 133 that celebrates how "good and pleasant" it is when "brothers" live together in unity. Having such a brother, the psalm affirms, is as luxurious as precious olive oil, or as refreshing as dew in the morning. These phrases do not mean to be fully free of tension, for the Bible knows very well about the reality of brothers, so consider,

> Cain and Abel,
> Jacob and Esau,
> David's sons,
> Absalom and Amnon in the parabolic allusion of 2 Samuel 14:4-11, and
> the prodigal son and older son in the parable of the two sons (Luke 15:11–32).

My brother Ed and I had our conflicts. The earliest conflict I can remember occurred when he was five and I was four. He locked himself into our old Chevrolet and would not let me in. My response was to break the car window that was not yet shatterproof. Our father did not look kindly upon my emancipatory act.

Mostly, we got along well. A year older, he was always a year ahead of me in school. But in our small school we were often in the same classroom. I recall in my sixth grade, we had "map study" in geography to see who could find locations on the map most quickly. Ed and I teamed together, dividing the map between us and so we often prevailed. We biked everywhere together, including the long mile uphill to school. We also practiced running each other off the road into the ditch on our bikes. We walked on stilts, he of course had the taller ones; we tried to push each other off our stilts.

In high school, we played basketball year round; our school was too small to have any other sport. We played pick-up games in the school gym on Sunday afternoons. Ed was a star player. He scored the winning free-throw in our tournament championship against Sweet Springs, a much larger school. He also led me into the world of work, so that I shared with him the rear end of a hay baler, together tying the wires of the bales.

He was a year ahead of me when he graduated from high school and went off to Elmhurst College. I missed him greatly during my senior year in high school. When I went off to Elmhurst the next year after my graduation, I was most conventionally quite frightened. Ed welcomed me, eased me in, and got me well-oriented for my four years there. He lettered in basketball at Elmhurst, and was a starter in his final two years. I was his very loud cheerleader. We more or less went our separate ways, as he was not exactly "study" oriented. But we did share work in the college kitchen where we bussed dishes together, and once a week mopped the dining room floor, large as it was. I recall that once the drycleaners in town completely burned up my treasured jacket. I was without any resource with which to respond to their careless destruction. But Ed, on my behalf, gave the cleaners a strong case of "what for." His vigorous response to my loss seemed to ease matters for me.

We went through the same process together at Eden Seminary where he preceded me by a year. He was helpful to me yet again, as I arrived at the seminary. Most especially he led me to my first "field work" assignment at Caroline Mission, an inner-city settlement house. While that assignment was for me quite awkward, Ed was at ease and prospered in the work. Indeed, he much preferred "field work" to the kind of book study on which I thrived. He was yet again a year ahead of me, until he took a "clinical year" of field education in a local congregation. As a result, we were together in our senior year at the seminary and shared some classes together, notably on the book of Romans taught by Richard Scheef. We graduated together.

By the time we graduated Ed had married Lu Ann Gleiber who was a nurse at Deaconess Hospital in St. Louis, Missouri. Promptly after graduation he and I were ordained together on June 29, 1958, by our father at St. Paul's Church in Blackburn, Missouri, our hometown. The ordination service, preached by Professor Ernest Nolte, was a happy time for our family, and my father swelled with pride. After that, Ed and I mostly went our separate ways, as I went off to graduate study at Union Seminary. We were never alienated from each other, but separated by work, geography and, of course, our growing families. We stayed in good touch, albeit mostly at my initiative. Ed subsequently served as pastor of two congregations, in Napoleon, Missouri and Lebanon, Illinois. He then joined the staff of the Illinois South Conference of the newly formed United Church of Christ. From there he became a Conference Minister in the New Hampshire Conference where he had a long, distinguished, and effective ministry. He especially thrived in the seventies when the church, of necessity, was pushed to rethinking its life and work, and so open to more experimentation. He was, as always, restless with conventional matters and ready to try something new.

Ed had many gifts that I did not. He was a superb manager and organizer, filled with great practical wisdom, overflowing with street smarts. Always decisive, as he aged he became more brusque and impatient. Through it all, he had a generous heart. He was strikingly progressive in his ideas. He once gave a lecture entitled, "In support of a very good word: Liberal."

Because I had considerable vocational success and enjoyed some visibility in church circles, I suspect that Ed regarded me as a "favorite" who was privileged beyond him. In retrospect I think that this perspective is to some point correct. We never talked about such matters, and we should have. But we finished well together. Tia and I went to see him in his last days after Lu had died. I finish with great *respect* for Ed and his many gifts that I did not possess. I finish with deep *gratitude* for the many ways he looked after me, cared for me, and supported me. And I finish with considerable *regret* that I did not do anything to redress his sense of diminishment by my more visible accomplishments. I have no doubt that had we talked honestly, we would have reached fresh levels of well-being together.

For now I will let the psalm ring in my ears with gratitude to God for him. He was for me like poured out olive oil, as he cared for me. He was for me like mountain dew to have him look after me. Maybe it is ever like that with brothers, grateful but with a flow of wistfulness for even more. I think more about our accidental disequilibrium as I ponder my own sons Jim and John who do not have an easy time together, one a successful businessman, the other an established academic.

I finish with the citation of a poem by John Greenleaf Whittier that became a hymn familiar in my childhood, "O Brother Man," *The Evangelical Hymnal*, 323:

O brother man, fold to thy heart thy brother;
For where love dwells, the peace of God is there;
To worship rightly is to love each other,
Each smile a hymn, each kindly deed a prayer.

We no longer sing that hymn, given its gender specificity. The sentiment of the poem, however, is to the point. My brother Ed, in his liberal, practical propensity, would have celebrated the hymn. Ed would have, in his low-church inclination, readily taken smiles and kindly deeds as hymns and prayers. He and I did not fully measure up, together, but our memory throbs with good passion, attentive care, and deep affection. The psalmist would have been glad for the life we have lived together. Our parents were proud of us, even while they wisely understood the fractured quality of all such relations.

14

NEW GODS!

IT IS STAGGERING to ponder the opportunity and freedom to choose "new gods." Such choosing requires the renunciation and rejection of old gods as inadequate and unreliable and inclined to oppressiveness. My comment on the notion of "new gods" is in three parts.

First, Israel in the Old Testament is a new people in world history whose identity is in response to and trust in YHWH, the God who rescued them from slavery in Egypt. Israel was not formed as a people until its emancipation and covenant-making at Sinai (Exod 19–24). Israel has a long tradition of needing to choose and re-choose to trust in, rely on, and obey the God of the Exodus. Early on, in the new land Joshua could summon his community to such a decision. The urgency and immediacy of such a decision is because loyalty to this God in every circumstance is one of freedom or oppression, of life or death (see Deut 30:15):

> *Not with our ancestors did the Lord make this covenant, but with us, who are all of us here alive today.* (Deut 5:3)

Thus Joshua could issue a summons in his circumstance:

> *Now therefore revere the Lord, and serve him in sincerity and in faithfulness; put away the gods that your ancestors served beyond the River and in Egypt, and serve the Lord. Now if are you are unwilling to serve the Lord, choose this day whom you will serve, whether the gods your ancestors served in the region beyond the River or the gods of the Amorites in whose*

> *land you are living; but as for me and my household, we will serve the Lord.* (Josh 24:14–15)

For now I am persuaded that the "conquest" of the land of promise was a revolt by oppressed peasants who were exploited by the urban elites who are labeled "Canaanites." Thus the summons of Joshua is to reject the gods who legitimated the exploitative economic system, and to pledge loyalty to the God of emancipation who is in contradiction to the gods of exploitation. The choice of "a new god" by Israel under the leadership of Joshua evoked in the books of Joshua and Judges massive retaliation against the "Canaanites" and their totems of exploitation. The account in Joshua can detail the extreme violence wrought by the peasants against their overlords. The Israelites, empowered by YHWH, acted against the city states. Those cities were citadels of exploitative violence and for that reason must be destroyed. In the same way, Elijah put before Israel a sharp either/or concerning the god of the urban elites (Baal) and the God, YHWH, the God of emancipation:

> *How long will you limp along with two different opinions? If the Lord is God, follow him; but if Baal, then follow him.* (1 Kgs 18:21)

The contest at Mount Carmel exalts the rainmaking power of YHWH, the Lord of creation, who is contrasted with the feeble, dysfunctional Baal.

The matter is given sharp articulation in the Song of Deborah (Judges 5). This early extended poem features the God from Seir (Sinai) who causes rain and earthquakes (vv. 4–5). Deborah and Barak sing of Israel's prosperity and success with the affirmation that "new gods" were "chosen" (v. 8). Israel embraced the storm-God of Sinai and rejected the gods of Sisera and his "Canaanite" ilk:

> *When new gods were chosen,*
> *then war was in the gates.*

> *Was shield or spear to be seen among forty thousand in*
> *Israel?*
> *My heart goes out to the commanders of Israel*
> *who offered themselves willingly among the people.*
> *Bless the Lord.* (v. 8)

It follows, in the poem and in the life of Israel, that the embrace of YHWH filled Israel's warriors with courage and eventually with a great victory. That great victory, according to the poem, is solely due to the power and engagement of the great creator God who fought against Sisera and the Canaanites with all the resources of creation, including the stars and torrents of rain:

> *The stars fought from heaven,*
> *from their courses they fought against Sisera.*
> *The torrent of Kishon swept them away,*
> *the onrushing torrent, the torrent of Kishon.*
> *March on, my soul, with might!* (vv. 20–21)

Jael is featured as a woman of great courage who was able to prevail even against the Canaanite general (vv. 26–27). The weak Israelites are mightily empowered by the embrace of YHWH, so much so that we are made witnesses to the sorry ending of Sisera and his company (vv. 28–30).

This breathtaking articulation makes clear that the "choice of YHWH" greatly impacted the socioeconomic and political practices of Israel. The poem attests to the truth of Karl Marx's belated aphorism:

> *The criticism of heaven is thus transformed into the criticism of earth, the criticism of religion into the criticism of law, and the criticism of heaven into the criticism of politics. (David McLellan,* The Thought of Karl Marx: An Introduction, 1971, p. 22)

That is, *religious claims* have a decisive impact for *the ordering of public life* in the world. Or conversely, Marx might have judged we could start with *the public life of the world* and reason backward to the *agency of God.* Thus the great victory of Israel is in real life, but the ultimate agent for the victory is YHWH, the God whom Israel has yet again embraced. Long before Marx, John Calvin begins his Institutes with the same awareness. Calvin begins his testimony with "knowledge of God." But he acknowledges that such knowledge begins in self-awareness:

> *No one can look upon himself without immediately turning his thoughts to the contemplation of God, in whom he "lives and moves" (Acts 17:28). . . . Accordingly, the knowledge of ourselves not only arouses us to seek God, but also, as it were, leads us by the hand to find him. Again, it is certain that man never achieves a clear knowledge of himself unless he has first looked on God's face, and then descends from contemplating him to scrutinize himself* (Institutes of Christian Religion Book 1, chapter 1, 35–27).

Thus Deborah and Barak can see that the "new God" led to Israel's victory. Conversely, one might begin with Israel's victory and reason back to the "new God" now chosen. Thus Deborah and Barak, and Calvin and Marx after them, insist on this deep linkage between the agency of God and our life in the world. One can begin either way, and reason to the other. Deborah and Barak have no doubt that Israel's success, prosperity, and victory result from God's rule. It is for good reason that Israel saw that emancipation and well-being necessitated a break with the gods who legitimated the "Canaanite" practice of exploitation.

This linkage is elemental for faithful living, even though we habitually seek to deny the connection, opting for the gifts of YHWH, but not responding to their source. That disconnect is later recognized by the prophet, Hosea, who sees that Israel has thanked the wrong gods (Hosea 2:8). Israel mistakenly judged that well-being came from Baal. Joshua, Elijah, and here Deborah and Barak know very well that Baal cannot and does not give good gifts. That is why we sing:

> *All good gifts are sent from heaven above.*
> *O thank the Lord, O thank the Lord,*
> *for all his love.*

We affirm that the good gifts of our lives are from the creator God. We boldly deny that such gifts could be given from elsewhere. The covenanted people of YHWH are always again needing to choose this "new god" who overcomes oppressive systems and makes prosperity possible.

The warriors of Israel, energized by YHWH and celebrated by Deborah and Barak, struggled mightily against the "Canaanite" power of the urban elites. Thus the narratives that follow this poem in Judges attest to the recurring defeat of the oppressive overlords, notably by Gideon. For good reason, the much later writer can celebrate this company of those empowered by YHWH:

> *And what more should I say? For time would fail me to tell of Gideon, Barak, Samson, Jephthah, of David and Samuel and the prophets—who through faith conquered kingdoms, administered justice, obtained promises, shut the mouths of lions, quenched raging fire, escaped the edge of the sword, won strength out of weakness, became mighty in war, put foreign armies to flight.* (Heb 11:32–34)

Once YHWH is chosen and Israel is empowered, brave emancipatory action is possible as human emancipators trust fully in the will and purpose of YHWH. Judges, from the poem to the narratives, witnesses to the deep, decisive impact of theological reality on the public life of the world.

Second, I was alerted to this matter of "new god" as I read *The Black Jacobins: Toussaint L'Ouverture and the San Domingo Revolution* (1963) by C. L. R. James. James traces the difficult, contested route whereby Haiti threw off the colonial rule of France and became a nation of free people. The primary agent of this emancipation from colonialism, as James shows clearly, was Toussaint L'Ouverture, a colored slave who became the undisputed leader of revolutionary emancipation who wisely and boldly mobilized his people to liberating action.

The decisive agency of Toussaint is beyond question. But at the same time James is attentive to theological reality. This is the prayer the slaves recited:

> *The god who created the sun which gives us light, who rouses the waves and rules the storm, though hidden in the clouds, he watches us. He sees all that the white man does. The god of the white man inspires him with crime, but our god calls upon us to do good works. Our god who is good to us orders us to avenge our wrongs. He will direct our arms and aid us. Throw away the symbol of the god of the whites who has so often caused us to weep, and listen to the voice of liberty, which speaks in the hearts of us all.* (p. 87)

James writes of the slaves:

> *They knew that as long as these plantations stood their lot would be to labour on until they dropped.* (p. 88)

Behind bold human agency was the act whereby a "new god" was chosen. The revolution was, however, grounded beyond strategy in faith. James contrasts two gods, the creator god and the god of the white man. The god of the white man, into whose sphere the vulnerable Blacks had been seduced, gives sanction for a brutal exploitative system of plantation labor. As long as Black slaves adhered to the god of white political power and exploitation, such exploitation appeared to be not only legitimate but beyond question.

The embrace of this "new god" led to two realities. First, it evoked violent rejection of the totems of this god. Thus emancipation required the destruction of the legitimating symbols of the plantation system. Second, it led to vengeance against the plantation owners and thus brutality. The two go hand in hand, *symbols* and *political, economic realities*. We are able to see in Haiti a reiteration and re-performance of the narrative of Joshua. A *new theological choice* evoked *new practice* on the ground. So Calvin understood that "knowledge of God" would lead to emancipatory fidelity. So Marx understood that critical awareness of the things of heaven, of religion, and of theology must, of necessity, lead to critical awareness of the earth, the law, and politics, that is, the constraints and vehicles whereby power and meaning are to be enacted. In Haiti the slaves became alert to emancipatory possibility when they perceived the will and power of "the god who created the sun" who readily outflanks the capacity of the god of the white man. As James articulates it, that critical awareness arose through singing, dancing, rites, and the generation of a zone of freedom that was outside the governance of the god of the white man. (It is no wonder, in the old South of the United States, that white plantation owners practiced careful supervision of the worship of colored slaves.) It is the capacity of the "new god" to evoke critical awareness that leads to emancipatory action. So it was in the days of Deborah and Barak as in the days of Toussaint L'Ouverture.

Third, I have pondered how this pattern of *new god-restorative action* might pertain to our social context, as to the social contexts of Pharaoh and the slaves in ancient Israel and colonialists and Black slaves in Haiti. To consider this matter we may begin with a critical reflection on the "old gods" that flourish among us. I could think of four such gods among us:

- There is *the god of the state* who endorses the status quo of power arrangements, and who is the author of capitalist ideology. This god, not unlike the god of the Solomonic temple, is a legitimator of the present order (see 1 Kgs 8:12–13).

- There is *the god of the philosophers* who is marked by omnipotence, omnipresence, and omniscience, who is unmoved and incapable of pathos.
- There is *the Jesus of evangelicalism* who in a transactional process has created salvation for those who believe.
- There is *the god of progressives*, a god who tilts toward unengaged deism, who authorizes the world and then summons us to do the work of redemption and reconciliation.

One can readily note that in this index of gods, there is no god who exercises emancipatory agency in the world. Thus these gods, in their several manifestations, are objects to be adored and relied upon, but from whom we can expect no newness. The church, moreover, variously colludes with these tiresome articulations of a god who matters very little in the life of the world.

In the face of such theological reductionism, the "new god" whom the church may choose and embrace is a God of transformative agency in the world. Against the "omni" metaphors, this God is capable of pathos, of being moved by the suffering of the world. Against the remote god of the state, this God is fully engaged on behalf of needy suffering people, and so on occasion against the status quo that produces and sustains suffering and misery. Against the transactionalism of some evangelicals, this God is dialogical, can be impinged upon, and can be summoned into circumstances of crises. Against the deism of some progressives, this God is an active agent in the socioeconomic, political life of the world. This "new God" does not live by and through syllogisms and formulas, but by and through narratives that celebrate specific interventions and transformations, and by and through song and poetry that refuse our most reliable explanatory practices of certitude. This new God lives in the singing of the congregation, is addressed by the prayers of the congregation, and is received from the lips of the preacher. The practice of narrative, song, and poem, unlike syllogism and formula, allows for the freedom of God to be engaged with the world in emancipatory and summoning ways. Thus I suggest that when the church has courage about its claims, nerve about its life, and honesty about the woundedness of the world, it may indeed choose this God. We may stand in the procession of Joshua who summoned Israel to "choose this day." We may follow in the narrative of Elijah in his uncompromising either/or. We may, after the manner of the disciples, "follow" him in glad obedience . . . unless we have "great possessions" (Mark 10:22). We may be in the company of Deborah and Barak in choosing a new God.

When *the new God* is chosen, it follows that there will be *restorative action.* Thus the peasants in Israel, after Deborah and Barak, refused and rejected exploitative power, and sought to reorder society in covenantal-egalitarian ways. The slaves of Haiti, after Toussaint, sought to reorder their society against colonial exploitation in the interest of freedom. And now we may ask about transformations evoked by the new God of emancipatory agency for those who sign on in faith. The response to this new God in ancient Israel and in Haiti led to revolutionary violence. It may indeed be that in extreme and unbearable circumstances of abuse and exploitation the response will inescapably be one of violence. So it was on January 6, 2021, with the mob doing its destructive work. But response to this new God need not be one of violence. It can be, rather, one of sober and disciplined justice. Thus the prophets of ancient Israel trace out responsive obedience to this new God of covenant in terms of justice, righteousness, steadfast love, faithfulness, and compassion (see Hos 2:19–20). Or in the categories of the apostle Paul, response to this new God is one of transformation (Rom 12:1), that issues in generosity (v. 7), hospitality (v. 13), solidarity (vv. 15–16), and a resolve to "overcome evil with good" (v. 21). Read through the prophetic repertoire and the index of Paul, a response to this new God in violence is incongruent with the character of God, even if on occasion circumstance evokes such destructive action.

The parallel between *the new God of Deborah and Barak* and *the sky God* of the slaves in Haiti invites us to relish and embrace the new God who is filled with grace and truth. It is precisely the agency of this new God that evokes a new agency among us for transformative, restorative action. It is the work of the church, in its witness and worship, to make this new God available and credible, in order that we may stake our lives on the faithfulness of God who is among us. So says the good preacher, so says the congregation in its singing, so says the assembly that prays boldly, in freedom for the newness of the world.

15

WE COUNT OUR DAYS

HAVING JUST TURNED ninety I have had ample time to ponder old age, growing old, and death. I find that the old age part sneaks up on me. Maybe, as the TV ad has it, "Age is simply a number." But I think not. It is our best human way of marking our reliance on God's grace and living it back to God in gratitude as best we can. Jenifer Senior, "The Age in Our Head," (*Atlantic* 2023, pp. 14–16) observes that most people think of themselves as twenty years younger than they are. But before she finishes her piece, she concludes:

> *I was struck by how many people said that their present age was their favorite one. A reassuring number of respondents [to a questionnaire] didn't want to trade their hard-earned wisdom—or humility, or self-acceptance, whatever they had accrued along the way—for some earlier moment.*

While I sometimes wish I were younger, I do not spend any time imagining that I am. In any case, this is a report on my pondering. In case it may interest you or be useful for your own pondering, here is an inventory of biblical texts that have been useful for me as the years have piled up.

We may most beneficially turn to Psalm 90 for our consideration of God's grace and our gratitude. After God has bid us to "turn back" (v. 3), the psalmist dares to spin the same imperative back to God: "Turn, O Lord!" (v. 13) The petition is that God should turn away from wrath, anger, or absence to enact compassion and steadfast love. The psalmist has the freedom and courage to address God in an imperative and to speak back to God the same imperative. It is the sway we may have in our most intimate relationships.

Two familiar phrases draw our attention. In verse 10, the psalmist voices realism about his life-span:

> *The days of our life are seventy years,*
> *or perhaps eighty, if we are strong.* (v. 10)

The psalmist sees that all around people die at those ages. And while our medical advances have upped that number significantly, the reality of these lines rings true. Life remains short. Bodies give in. We die. There is no escape. But the verse adds even more reality:

> *Even then their span is only toil and trouble;*
> *they are soon gone, and we fly away.* (v. 10)

The years we live overflow with endless vexation and work. No matter how much we succeed with wisdom, wealth, or power, human life consists in demands and anxieties. The next verse, moreover, assigns such burdens to the imposition of God. It is for that reason that the psalmist addresses God, asks God to turn and relieve the pressure that belongs intrinsically to the human condition. Thus the psalmist knows and tells us that life at its most extended is not and will not be a zone of unqualified well-being, even as much as we hope and pray that it might be.

The other most familiar phrase is in verse 12:

> *So teach us to count our days*
> *that we may gain a wise heart.* (v. 12)

The word "count" or "number" merits attention. Clearly it does not mean simply to "enumerate" the sequence of days. That would be easy enough. My recent birthday card from the beloved William West and David Ellis reports that my ninety years is 32,850 days; so they are enumerated! (It also reports that it is 47,304,000 minutes!) Something more is required here. The verse means, rather, to slow down, to notice, to savor each day, and so face one's life with a capacity to see the present reality of life and the coming reality of death in a world well governed by God:

> *He petitions for a right wisdom about life, an ability to deal with the knowledge of death in such a way—beyond all categories, such as divine wrath or death as punishment for sin—that life can be accepted as a gift from God and lived as something fulfilled. Thus the petitioner asks that knowing about the limitedness of the time allotted to each person may make one aware of the immense value of every single day ("teach us to count our days!"), the* now *given one at each and every moment. In light of the knowledge of death, what is important, in the view of this petition, is to receive every individual instant, in astonishment, as a gift of a good creator God and to withstand the challenge of it. (Frank-Lothar Hossfeld and Erich* Zenger, Psalms 2: A Commentary on Psalms 51–100, Augsburg Fortress, 2005, 413)

The outcome of such intentionality may be a "wise heart."

> *The "wise heart" makes possible a view of the world that is realistic and affirmative of reality—even that of death. If "wisdom" means the art of living, then the ability here asked of God . . . to say yes to life and to live that yes (in the midst of many things that deserve a no) is Wisdom's art of living par excellence. (Hossfeld and Zenger,* Psalms 2, 432)

The psalmist has no yearning to wish death away, but intends to face it honestly, and so to see his life whole from beginning to end as a project in which the rule of God is powerfully at work. There is here no escapism and no romanticism, but the honest work of seeing one's life as it is in the context of God's governance. It is an act of theological realism.

But lest in my pondering of my life-span I be drawn too simplistically into the sphere of God's unmistakable governance, here are two other texts that sound a very different kind of realism. These are texts we do not often notice, but I have found that they merit our attention. The first of these texts is in Leviticus 27:1–7. These verses concern the monetary value of a human life (one's own or the life of one's child) offered to the service of God. (The remainder of this odd chapter concerns the price of an animal for sacrifice and the price of land.) The establishing of the monetary value of a human life evidences sober realism. It recognizes that a very young child or a very old person is of less value (and so a lower equivalence), because such persons cannot perform the required work so well. Thus the table of equivalences goes like this:

Age	**Male**	**Female**
20 to 60 years	50 shekels	30 shekels
5 to 20 years	20 shekels	10 shekels
Over 60 years	15 shekels	10 shekels
1 month to 5 years	5 shekels	5 shekels

(See Walter C. Kaiser, Jr., "The Book of Leviticus," NIB, p. 1187).

We are able to see the realism that old age lessens one's value because the potential for productive work diminishes. Thus it is a law of the marketplace that age diminishes monetary value. And certainly every aging person knows about the waning of energy and the loss of productive capacity. In this text we are clearly in a universe quite remote from the theological reality of Psalm 90. Now we deal with the recognition that the human person is *homo economicus*, a reality to be faced as we quibble about investment in the maintenance and support for us old people (Social Security and Medicare).

That honest recognition of the waning capacity of old age is articulated as well in the realism of Ecclesiastes 12:1–8. The teacher bids us to be glad in youth that is referred to the creator God. That wondrous season of youth is then contrasted with the disabilities that come with aging. Again, this is a voice of realism about physical loss that variously comes with old age. The words are these:

> *In the day when the guards of the house tremble, and the strong men are bent, and the women who grind cease working because they are few, and those who look through the windows see dimly; when the doors on the street are shut, and the sound of the grinding is low, and one rises up at the sound of a bird, and all the daughters of song are brought low; when one is afraid of heights, and terrors are in the road; the almond tree blossoms, the grasshopper drags itself along and desire fails; because all must go to their eternal home, and the mourners will go about the streets.* (Ecclesiastes 12:3–5)

These images are easily taken as reference to failing body parts:

> *keeper of the house;* arm
> *strong men bent;* legs
> *grinders;* teeth
> *windows;* eyes
> *doors;* ears
> *sound of grinding;* voice
> *almond tree blossoms;* gray hair
> *grasshopper drags along;* difficulty walking
> *(See Hans Walter Wolff,* Anthropology of the Old Testament, 1974, 123).

These verses have all body parts in purview. And for all our modern learning about health and self-care, these matters have not changed. Body parts wear out. You cannot fool your body (*nephesh*)! This sober recognition resonates with the script of monetary value in Leviticus 27. In old age we are diminished. Our value in a market economy subsides. For all our resolve and care, it comes upon us, until the ultimate reach of bodily diminishment, death!

The inventory of Ecclesiastes 12 is tersely echoed in the Fourth Gospel:

> *Very truly, I tell you, when you were younger, you used to fasten your own belt and to go wherever you wished. But when you grow old, you will stretch out your hands, and someone else will fasten a belt around you and take you where you do not wish to go.* (John 21:18)

In youth one has freedom and mobility. In old age, by contrast, one requires a minder who dresses you and takes you where you do not want to be. The image suggests old people who want only to be "at home," but are sometimes against their will institutionalized for "better care." To be sure, the Fourth Gospel's usage of this imagery has no interest in the diminishment of old age. Rather, the verse is on its way to verse 19, wherein suffering for the gospel leads to *the loss of agency* as the hostile empire imposes its will upon the faithful. It is unmistakable that the "follow me" by Jesus in this verse is the most dangerous imperative we will ever hear.

The juxtaposition of these texts is telling. On the one hand, "seventy or perhaps eighty years with trouble," and "count our days"; on the other hand, waning monetary value and bodily dysfunction. The texts converge in their testimony to our mortality and with a poignant reference to God who, unlike us, is "Immortal, Invisible, God only wise." Thus in Ecclesiastes, the "breath" (*ruah*) returns to God who gave it (12:7). While the sacrificial system of Leviticus 27 may assert equivalences for human persons, in the end the human person can have no monetary equivalence, no monetary value, but only reliance on the "favor of the Lord our God" (Psalm 90:17). (Efforts at monetary equivalence for human persons are evident in the inventories of Ezekiel 27:13 and Revelation 18:14 that easily arrive at a sale price for slaves. Just as we have done in our own slave economy in the United States.)

Finally I thought of two other texts that push the boundary of aging to its extreme. The words of Hosea are familiar to us only because Paul quotes them:

Shall I ransom them from the power of Sheol?
Shall I redeem them from Death?
O Death, where are your plagues?
O Sheol, where is your destruction?
Compassion is hidden from my eyes. (Hosea 13:14)

The intent of Hosea is very different from that of Paul in his quote of these lines. In the prophet, God asks two rhetorical questions that require negative answers:

No, I will not ransom them from the power of Sheol.
No, I will not redeem them from the God of Death (Mot).

The two vocatives, "O Death (*Mot*), O Sheol" are summons to these negative powers (that are answerable to God) to work their worst. The poet finds divine compassion hidden and elusive. This is a very hard saying, that God will mobilize the powers of Death against recalcitrant Ephraim. Death is at the beck and call of God! The only possible good news here is that Death is not an autonomous agent, but is subject to the governance of God.

A Christian, however, does not read these lines in Hosea apart from their quote in 1 Corinthians wherein Paul celebrates the victory God has won over *Mot* in the resurrection of Jesus:

For this perishable body puts on imperishability, and this mortal body puts on immortality, then the saying that is written will be fulfilled:

Death has been swallowed up in victory.
Where, O death, is your victory?
Where, O death, is your sting?

The sting of death is sin, and the power of sin is the law. But thanks be to God, who gives us the victory through our Lord Jesus Christ. (1 Cor 15:54–57)

God has declared war on *Mot*. *Mot* has no victory. *Mot* has no sting. Because the God life has prevailed. The reality of "seventy or eighty years," the need to "count our days," the diminished capacity of the old, and the helplessness of the old are not denied. All of that is right before our eyes. It is, however, all put in context, and context alters everything. It turns out, in the proclamation of Paul, that death amounts to no substantive defeat for the purposes of God. There is no need for denial. The "perishable body" is marked by weakness. But that weakness is not the final truth of our life.

Finally, to return to Psalm 90. In verse 3, human persons are addressed as "mortals" (*'nosh*). The poet utilizes the term for humanity in its weakness, not *'adam*, humanity in its strength! These verses put humanity in proper perspective before the reality of God:

> *You turn us back to dust,*
> *and say, "Turn back, you* mortals*."*
> *For a thousand years in your sight*
> *are like yesterday when it is past,*
> *or like a watch in the night.*
> *You sweep them away; they are like a dream,*
> *like grass that is renewed in the morning;*
> *in the morning it flourishes and is renewed;*
> *in the evening it fades and withers.* (Psalm 90:3–6)

Or as Watts's hymn has it:

> *A thousand ages in thy sight are like an evening gone;*
> *Short as the watch that ends the night before the rising sun.*
> (Glory to God, 687)

Our humanity is ultimately transitory, like the flash of a light, like the flick of a switch, gone in an instant. We are like a dream . . . or a nightmare. We are like grass, only for a season, dependent on water and sun, and then dried up, cut down, forgotten. The psalm does not flinch from its truth-telling. In our frail short-term existence, we dwell amid the God who neither slumbers nor sleeps, who remembers and does not forget. Our finiteness remains our ongoing enigma. We juxtapose what we know of *our bodily reality* with what we know and trust of *the fidelity of God*. There is no settling between the two, because both are the reality of our life.

All of this I was pondering in the run-up to my ninetieth birthday. And then I celebrated. I had a large company of friends who celebrated with me. The celebration filled me with exultant gratitude. On that day I did not think much of my frail reality. But it was there as a truth of my life. As I have numbered my days, every one of them is filled with gratitude for a measure of good health, for a measure of meaningful work that persists, and for the immeasurable blessing of generous folk all around who bless me daily.

The day after my birthday, with Tia I watched a part of the Oscar awards on March 12. The movies celebrated on that night are variously equipped to be truth-telling about the human condition. That truth-telling is honest. On that night, however, not much of the truth-telling was in evidence. The evening featured handsome offers of beautiful human flesh, all with strutting and preening splendor. No hurt, no tears except tears of elation, no violence except filmed violence, no defect, no failure. All was well. In the wake of my ninetieth birthday, I wondered if this award ceremony was a pageant of *denial*, and that done by those who are so capable of presenting *reality* to us. Maybe there was some denial, because the beautiful people can do that for a season. My guess is that for the most part, they knew better. And for a moment—not unlike the moment of my birthday—they screened out the force of death for the sake of celebration and affirmation. We do that. We do that for each other, and for ourselves. No problem with such screening out as long as it is only a momentary yearning. As long as we know better. As long as we recognize our dream-like, grass-like morality. The beauty industry, the health industry, and the money industry all collude to imagine that we can be masters of our own fate. But we know better. That is why we count our days. That is why we know that our days have a finite number. That is why we know that every day is a gift; and we may count it and make it count. But we pause in our counting and in our making count, for the sake of sober reality. In that pause we may turn our attention away from our frailty to the God of all compassion. It is to this God that we voice our petition that God may let the work of our hands count for something:

> *Let the favor of the Lord our God be upon us,*
> *and prosper for us the work of our hands—*
> *O prosper the work of our hands!* (Psalm 90:17)